GOD'S FINAL WORD

Understanding The Church's Victory in Christ Through Revelation

Willie Harris, Jr.

Zion Media Publishing

God's Final Word: Understanding The Church's Victory in Christ Through Revelation

Copyright © 2025 by Willie Harris, Jr

Illustration © 2025 by Abigail Kristina Harris.
Design title: Revelation Throne (p.36)

Published by: Zion Media Publishing, www.zionmediapub.com

United States of America

All rights reserved under International Copyright Law. No part of this publication may be reproduced or transmitted in any form or by any means, electronic or mechanical - including photocopying, recording, or by any information storage and retrieval system - without permission in writing from the publisher.

Unless otherwise indicated, all Scriptures are taken from the The Holy Bible, English Standard Version, Copyright © 2001 by Crossway Bibles, a publishing ministry of Good News Publishers.

Paperback ISBN: 979-8-9990900-1-0
Hardback ISBN: 979-8-9990900-0-3
eBook ISBN: 979-8-9990900-2-7

Printed in the United States of America

This book was published with assistance of
Goodwill Media Services Corp, www.goodwillmediaservices.com.

Goodwill Media Services Corp.

TABLE OF CONTENTS

01   INTROUCTION

11   PART ONE:
     Meeting the Risen Christ (Revelation 1)

19   PART TWO:
     Letters to God's People (Revelation 2-3)

29   PART THREE:
     Heaven's Perspective (Revelation 4-7)

47   PART FOUR:
     Warning Trumpets (Revelation 8-11)

57   PART FIVE:
     Cosmic Battle (Revelation 12-14)

71   PART SIX:
     Final Victory (Revelation 15-22)

91   APPENDICES:
     A. Complete Symbol Reference Guide
     B. Timeline of Revelation Events
     C. Maps and Charts
     D. Personal Growth Resources

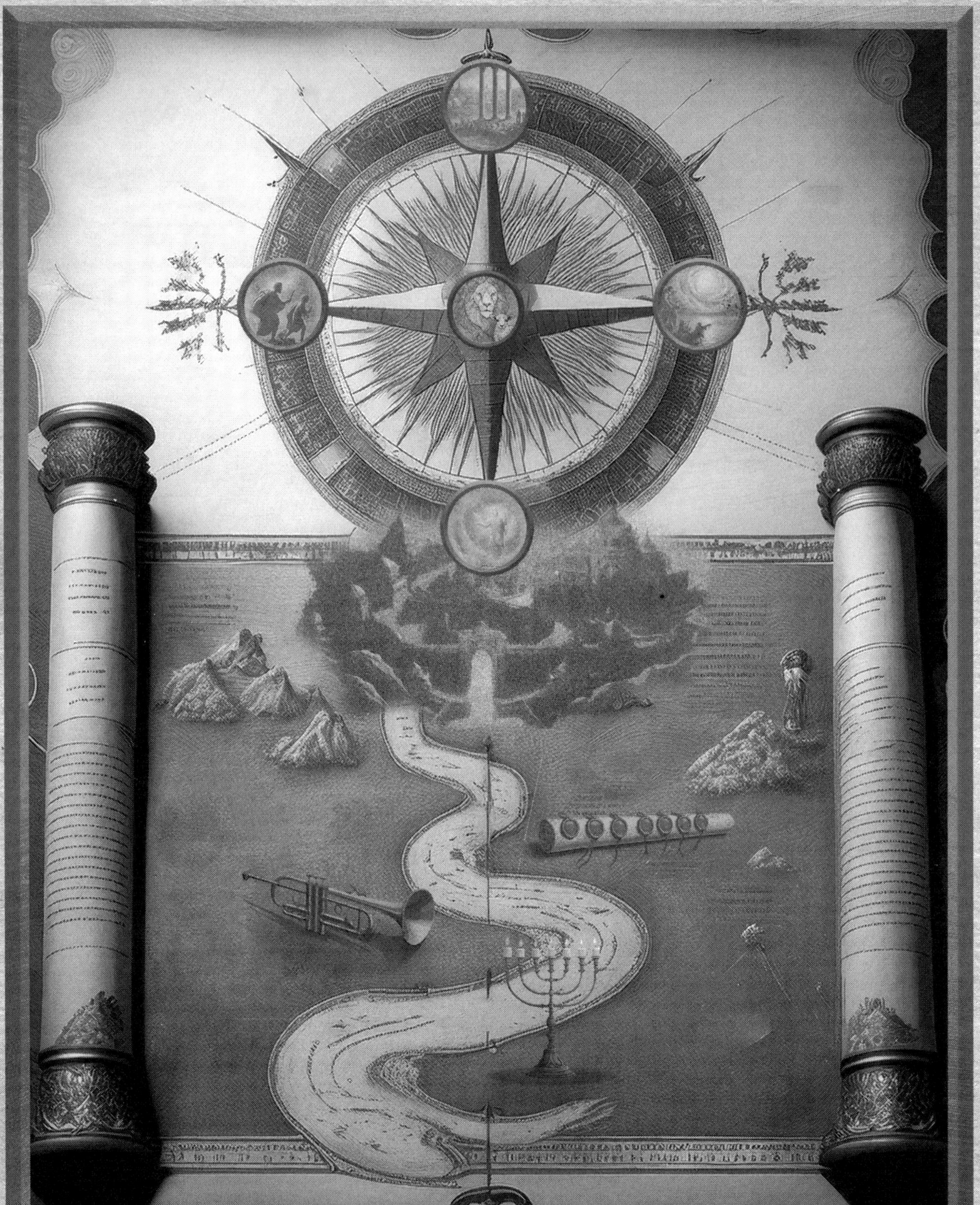

INTRODUCTION
PREPARING FOR THE JOURNEY

Welcome to Revelation

The final book of the Bible isn't meant to confuse or frighten us—it's meant to fill us with hope and inspire faithful worship. As you open these pages, you're beginning a journey that will deepen your understanding of God's ultimate victory and help you live confidently in light of His promises.

God's Heart Behind This Book

When the Apostle John received this revelation on the isle of Patmos, he wasn't given a complex puzzle to decode or a secret timeline to decipher. Instead, God gave him—and us—a powerful unveiling of Jesus Christ and His ultimate victory. This revelation was meant to encourage believers facing persecution and temptation to remain faithful, showing them that their temporary struggles would give way to eternal triumph.

The same message rings true for us today. In a world of increasing hostility toward faith, mounting cultural pressure to compromise, and the ever-present temptation to align with the values of our age, Revelation reminds us that Jesus reigns supreme. Every prophecy, symbol, and vision in this book ultimately points to this truth: Jesus wins, and His people win with Him.

THE PURPOSE AND PROMISE OF STUDY

Revelation 1:3 promises a special blessing for those who read, hear, and keep the words of this prophecy. This blessing comes through:

- **Seeing Jesus in His Glory:** While the Gospels show us Jesus in His humility, Revelation displays Him in His present majesty as the risen, reigning King.

- **Understanding Our Times:** Revelation provides the spiritual perspective needed to discern world events and live wisely.

- **Finding Strength for Today:** This book assures us that our faithfulness matters and our present struggles are temporary.

- **Living for Eternity:** As we grasp the eternal consequences of our choices, we're inspired to live more faithfully.

- **Growing in Worship:** Seeing Jesus as He truly is leads to deeper, more passionate worship.

HOW TO USE THIS BOOK

This book is designed to serve multiple purposes and can be used in several ways:

FOR PERSONAL STUDY

- Begin each chapter by reading the designated Scripture passage.
- Read through the chapter overview to grasp the big picture.
- Work through the verse-by-verse teaching at your own pace.
- Take time to reflect on the personal questions at the end.
- Use the prayer response to guide your time with God.
- Declare the victory truths in your own life.
- Refer to the appendices for deeper study on specific topics.

FOR GROUP STUDY AND TEACHING

- Have participants read the Scripture passage beforehand.
- Use the chapter overview as a starting point for discussion.
- Focus on 2-3 reflection questions that resonate with your group.
- Pray through the prayer response together.
- Declare the victory truths as a group confession.
- Utilize the Leader's Guide in Appendix D for additional questions.
- Reference the teaching outlines for presentation help.
- Draw from the historical backgrounds and word studies for context.

FOR TEACHING ANG PREACHING

- Each chapter is structured to easily convert to a message outline.
- Main headings work as sermon points.
- Teaching boxes provide additional illustrations.
- Reflection questions help develop application.
- Victory declarations serve as powerful conclusions.

Remember, the goal isn't just knowledge, but transformation. Don't rush through the material. Allow God's Spirit to speak to you through these ancient yet timeless words.

FOUNDATIONS FOR UNDERSTANDING

Different Views with Grace

Christians often interpret Revelation differently, but we can approach these differences with grace while focusing on our shared essentials. The major interpretive approaches include:

1 **Preterist View:** Most prophecies fulfilled in the first century.

2 **Historicist View:** Prophecies fulfilled throughout church history.

3 **Futurist View:** Most prophecies await future fulfillment.

4 **Idealist View:** Portrays timeless spiritual principles.

While interpretations vary, all orthodox views agree that:

- Jesus Christ is central to Revelation.
- God is sovereign over history.
- The church is called to faithful witness.
- Evil will ultimately be defeated.
- Jesus will return and make all things new.

TEACHING BOX: Four Views of Revelation

Preterist View (Past)

- Most prophecies fulfilled by 70 AD (Jerusalem's destruction) or by the fall of Rome.
- Revelation written primarily for its first-century audience.
- Historical context is essential for interpretation.

Historicist View (Progressive)

- Revelation forecasts entire church age.
- Often links prophecies to specific historical events.
- Sees ongoing fulfillment throughout church history.

Futurist View (Future)

- Most prophecies await future fulfillment.
- Often includes belief in a 7-year tribulation.
- Divides between pre-tribulation, mid-tribulation, and post-tribulation rapture views.

Idealist View (Principles)

- Sees Revelation as symbolic of the spiritual battle in every age.
- Revelation depicts recurring patterns throughout history.
- Emphasizes spiritual principles over specific predictions.

In this book, we'll primarily use the Idealist view while acknowledging insights from other perspectives.

READING APOCALYPTIC LITERATURE

Revelation uses apocalyptic language - a genre that employs symbols and visions to reveal spiritual realities. Understanding this genre is crucial for proper interpretation.

Symbolic Communication

- Numbers (7 = completeness, 12 = God's people)
- Colors (white = victory, red = blood/war)
- Objects (crowns = authority, throne = sovereignty)
- Heavenly visions revealing earthly realities

Interpretation Principles

- Interpret symbolically unless context demands literal.
- Follow the author's explanations of symbols.
- Keep the main message in focus.
- Connect to Old Testament imagery.

WORD STUDY: Apocalypse

The Greek word "apokalypsis" (ἀποκάλυψις) simply means "unveiling" or "revelation." While today we associate "apocalypse" with catastrophic end-of-the-world scenarios, the original meaning refers to pulling back the curtain to reveal what was previously hidden. Revelation is not primarily about destruction but divine disclosure—God revealing truths about Jesus Christ and ultimate reality that we couldn't know otherwise.

THE POWER OF SYMBOLS

Revelation is filled with vivid symbols that require careful interpretation. The book has 404 verses with 278 of those verses containing one or more Old Testament references—meaning over two-thirds of the book draws on earlier biblical imagery! Understanding these symbols is key to understanding the message.

- **Seven**—Represents completeness or perfection (seven churches, seven seals, seven trumpets, seven bowls).
- **Four**—Represents geographic completeness—the four corners of the earth.
- **Twelve**—Represents the completeness of God's people (twelve tribes, twelve apostles).
- **1,000**—Symbolizes a vast number, not necessarily a literal millennium.
- **144,000**—12 × 12 × 1,000 = completeness × completeness × vastness = all of God's
- people.
- **Beasts**—Represent political powers and empires.
- **Horns**—Symbolize strength and power.
- **Eyes**—Represent wisdom and insight.
- **White Robes**—Symbolize purity, victory, and divine vindication.

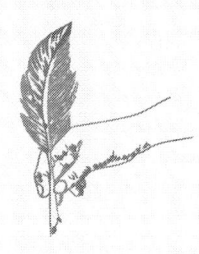

Remember, these symbols would have been more readily understood by first-century readers familiar with Old Testament imagery.

HISTORICAL CONTEXT

Understanding the first-century setting illuminates both the original message and its relevance today:

The Roman World

- Empire at its height of power and influence.
- Emperor worship becoming mandatory.
- Economic system increasingly tied to pagan practices.

The Church's Situation

- Facing external persecution from Rome.
- Dealing with internal compromise.
- Needing encouragement and hope.

HISTORICAL BACKGROUND: The Isle of Patmos

When John received this revelation, he was exiled on Patmos—a small, rocky island about 37 miles off the coast of Asia Minor (modern Turkey). This was not a vacation retreat but a Roman penal colony where prisoners were sent for exile and forced labor.

Patmos was a ten-by-six mile mountainous island in the Aegean Sea. Prisoners like John endured hard labor with insufficient food and clothing. Here, in this place of suffering, John received the most glorious vision in Scripture—a powerful reminder that God's revelations often come in our darkest moments.

Modern Parallels These pressures parallel our modern challenges:

- Cultural pressure to compromise.
- Economic consequences for faith.
- Social cost of following Christ.
- Need for hope in troubled times.

MOVING FORWARD

Remember, Revelation isn't primarily about decoding symbols or predicting dates—it's about seeing Jesus more clearly and living more faithfully in light of His coming victory. As we begin this journey together, let's approach it with hearts ready to worship and lives ready to be transformed.

> **"The revelation of Jesus Christ, which God gave him to show to his servants the things that must soon take place…"**
>
> **-Revelation 1:1 (ESV)**

Prayer Focus: Lord, as we begin this study of Revelation, give us wisdom to understand, hearts to receive, and courage to apply its truths. Help us see Jesus more clearly and live more faithfully as we explore this powerful book. Amen.

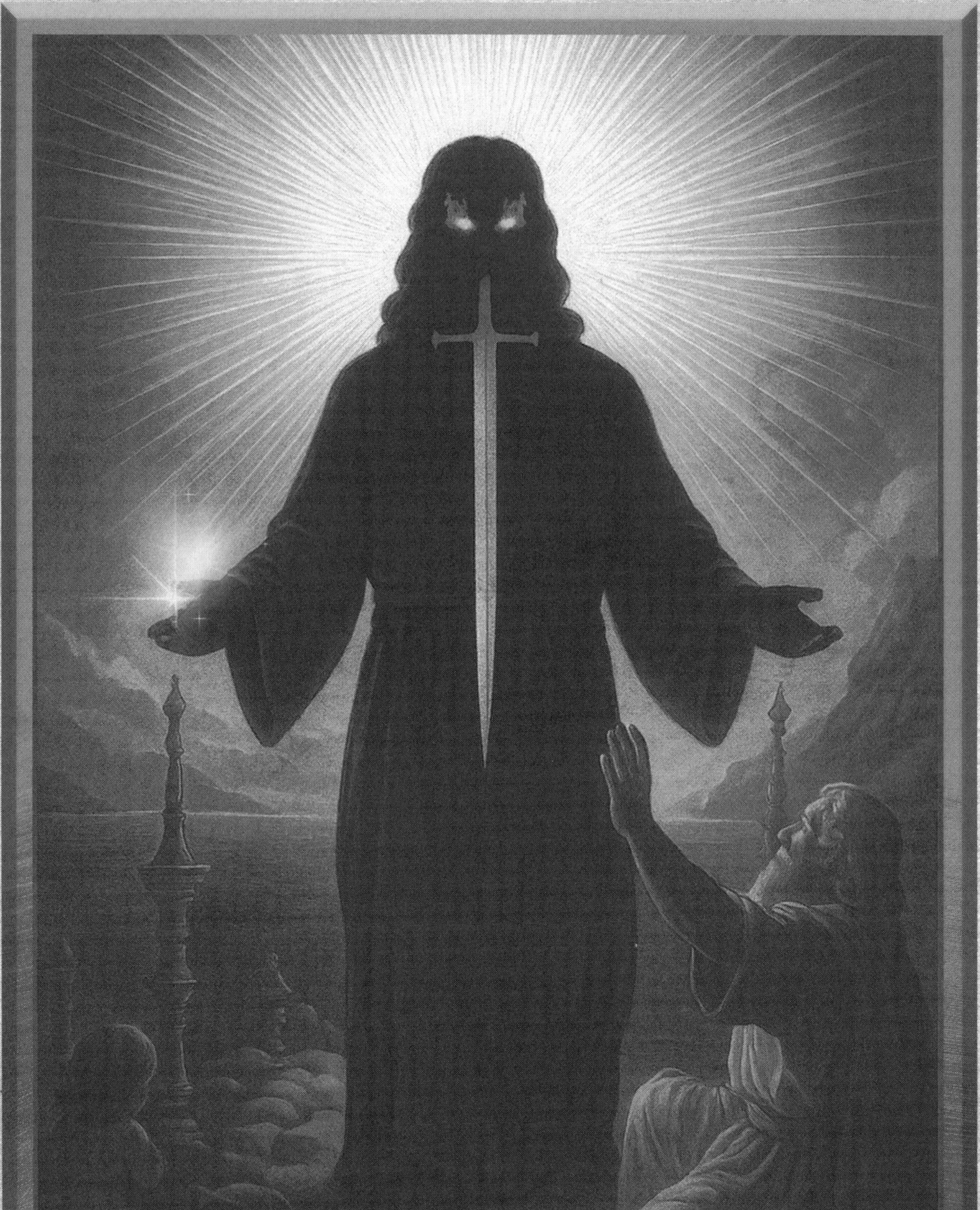

PART ONE

MEETING THE RISEN CHRIST (REVELATION 1)

Begin by reading Revelation 1:1-20

Making It Personal

When you hear the word "apocalypse," what comes to mind? Most of us immediately think of catastrophic destruction or the end of the world. But I want to share something transformative with you: the word "apocalypse" simply means "to reveal" or "unveil." This book isn't primarily about destruction—it's about revelation. We're about to witness Jesus Christ unveiled in His full glory.

The Great Unveiling

God has orchestrated this revelation through a remarkable chain of communication. Like a perfectly delivered message, it flows from God the Father, through Jesus Christ, is carried by His angel, entrusted to John, and finally delivered to us—God's servants. The Greek word used here for "made it known" actually means "to give a sign." This tells us something crucial about how to read Revelation—it's communicated primarily through signs and symbols.

You might wonder about the phrase "soon to take place" since we're reading these words two thousand years later. Here's the key: since Christ's first coming, we've been living in the final chapter of God's story. These aren't just the end times—they're the times of fulfillment, when God's promises are actively unfolding in history. When Christ returns, all of human history as we know it will be over.

God pronounces a threefold blessing in this book: for those who read it aloud (especially important when most people couldn't read), for those who hear it read, and—most importantly—for those who keep what is written in it. The greatest blessing isn't in satisfying our curiosity about the future—it's in allowing these words to transform how we live today. The time is near, and John writes this revelation to encourage believers facing both threats and seductions to remain faithful to Christ.

CROSS REFERENCE: First Gospel Promise

The unveiling of Jesus Christ in Revelation completes what God began in Genesis 3:15, where He promised that the offspring of the woman would crush the serpent's head. This "proto-evangelium" (first gospel) finds its ultimate fulfillment in Jesus's victory over Satan as revealed in Revelation. From the first book to the last, the Bible tells one unified story of God's redemptive plan through Jesus Christ.

JESUS AMONG HIS CHURCHES

When John addresses seven churches in Asia Minor (modern-day Turkey), he's doing more than sending a regional letter. The number seven in Scripture represents completion or perfection. These seven historical churches represent every type of church in every generation. When we read about these churches, we're reading about ourselves.

Notice how grace and peace flow from the complete Trinity: From the Father—"who is, who was, and who is to come." People thought Rome would reign forever. But Rome has fallen, while God remains eternal. Nations rise and fall, but God endures.

From the "seven spirits" before His throne—if we took this literally, we'd have nine persons in the Godhead! Instead, the seven spirits represent the Holy Spirit's perfect, complete work. He is all-present and all-seeing.

From Jesus Christ, described in three powerful titles:

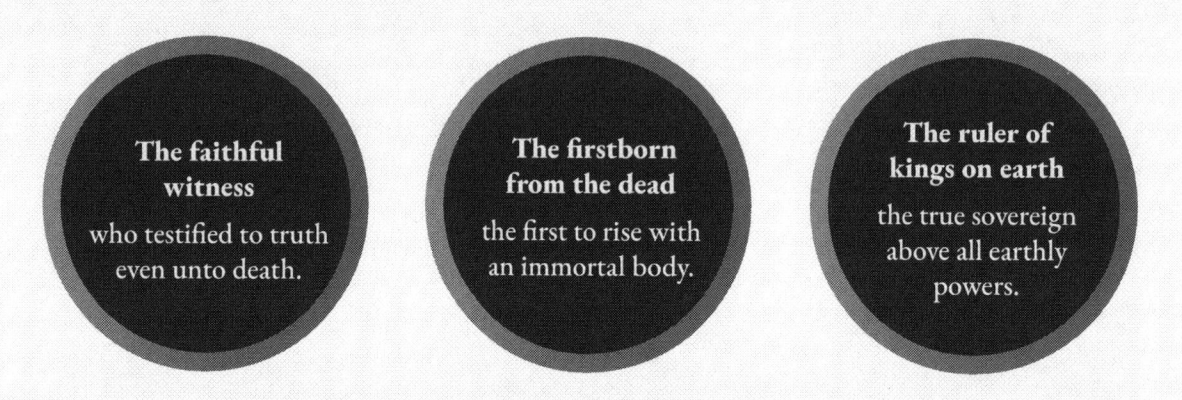

- **The faithful witness** who testified to truth even unto death.
- **The firstborn from the dead** the first to rise with an immortal body.
- **The ruler of kings on earth** the true sovereign above all earthly powers.

This Jesus has done something remarkable for us. He has freed us from our sins by His blood and made us into a kingdom of priests to God. Think about that! We who were once slaves to sin have been freed and given a royal priesthood.

WORD STUDY: Firstborn from the Dead

When Revelation calls Jesus "the firstborn from the dead," it uses the Greek term "prōtotokos" (πρωτότοκος), which signifies preeminence and priority—not merely chronological order. Jesus wasn't literally the first person ever resurrected (Elijah and Elisha raised the dead in the Old Testament, and Jesus Himself raised Lazarus), but He is the first to rise with a glorified, immortal body, never to die again. As "firstborn," Jesus is both preeminent over death and the pioneer of resurrection, guaranteeing that all who are in Him will follow in His pattern with resurrected bodies that will never grow old or die.

THE GLORY OF CHRIST

Let me take you to Patmos, where John first received this vision. This wasn't a peaceful retreat—it was a Roman penal colony where prisoners endured hard labor with insufficient food and clothing. Yet here, in this place of exile and hardship, John was "in the Spirit on the Lord's Day." Even in tribulation, he continued to worship.

Suddenly, John hears a voice like a trumpet and turns to see something that would forever change how we see Jesus. The vision begins with seven golden lampstands—representing the churches—and among them stands One like a son of man. This title reaches back to Daniel's prophecy where one like a son of man receives an eternal kingdom from the Ancient of Days.

The vision is overwhelming in its detail and significance:

- His robe reaching to His feet with a golden sash—marking Him as our royal high priest.
- Hair white like wool—showing His eternal wisdom.
- Eyes blazing like flames of fire—penetrating every heart with perfect judgment.
- Feet like bronze refined in a furnace—displaying His unshakeable strength and stability.
- Voice thundering like mighty waters—carrying ultimate authority.
- Seven stars in His right hand—holding complete authority over His church.
- A sharp two-edged sword from His mouth—His Word that both saves and judges.
- Face shining like the sun in full strength—revealing His unveiled glory.

Each detail reveals something profound about who Jesus is. This isn't just poetry—it's theology in high definition. The humble carpenter from Nazareth now stands revealed as the glorious King of kings.

HISTORICAL BACKGROUND: Son of Man

When Jesus is called "one like a son of man," this directly references Daniel 7:13–14, where Daniel sees "one like a son of man coming with the clouds of heaven" who receives an everlasting dominion from the Ancient of Days. This was a messianic title pointing to the heavenly, eternal nature of the Messiah.

Jesus frequently referred to Himself as "the Son of Man" (over 80 times in the Gospels), making it His favorite self-designation. This title simultaneously conveyed His genuine humanity and His divine authority. In Revelation, we see this title fulfilled as Jesus appears in glory, having received the kingdom promised in Daniel's vision.

FIRST VISION IMPACT

How did John—the beloved disciple who had once leaned against Jesus' chest at the Last Supper—respond to this overwhelming vision? He fell at Christ's feet as though dead. When faced with the unveiled glory of Jesus, there's no room for casual familiarity. This is a sobering reminder for us in an age when we sometimes treat Jesus more like a buddy than the Lord of glory.

But watch what happens next. Jesus places His right hand on John and speaks those precious words: "Fear not." The same hand that holds the seven stars now rests on His trembling servant. Then Jesus identifies Himself with three powerful declarations: He is the First and the Last, the Living One who died but is now alive forevermore, and the One who holds the keys of Death and Hades.

These aren't just titles—they're promises. When Jesus says He is the First and the Last, He's telling us that nothing exists outside His authority. When He declares Himself the Living One, He's reminding us that His resurrection isn't just a past event but a present reality. And when He shows us the keys of Death and Hades, He's assuring us that He has absolute authority over humanity's greatest enemies.

Keys symbolize authority and access. When Jesus rose from the dead, He took the keys from death and Satan. Even if the ruling powers of this world throw us into death's prison, Jesus will let us out because He has the keys! Death has no power over the believer; therefore, we have no reason to fear.

OUR RESPONSE TODAY

How should this vision of Christ shape our lives today? When we gather for worship, we're not just singing songs—we're standing in the presence of the One whose face shines like the sun. When we read His Word, we're hearing the voice that sounds like rushing waters. When we face opposition, we're following the One who holds all authority in heaven and on earth.

Let me ask you something personal: How does this vision of Jesus compare with how you usually think about Him? What would change in your life if you consistently remembered that this glorious Christ walks among us?

The challenges facing the first-century church might seem distant, but we face our own versions today:

- Where they faced emperor worship, we face the idolatry of self, success, and material comfort.
- Where they faced persecution for not participating in pagan rituals, we face pressure to conform to secular values.
- Where they were tempted to compromise their faith for economic gain, we face similar choices in our workplaces.

The same Jesus who appeared to John in such overwhelming glory says to us today, "Fear not." Whether you're facing persecution, temptation, doubt, or despair, this vision offers both comfort and challenge. Comfort, because He holds all authority and walks among us. Challenge, because such a glorious Lord deserves our complete devotion.

Jesus instructed John to "write, therefore, what you have seen, what is now and what will take place later" (v.19). This threefold division helps us understand the structure of Revelation:

- "What you have seen" - The vision of the glorified Christ (chapter 1)
- "What is now" - The messages to the seven churches (chapters 2–3)
- "What will take place later" - The prophetic visions (chapters 4–22)

Remember, we're not just reading an ancient vision—we're encountering the living Christ. Let this revelation of His glory strengthen you for whatever challenges you face. The One who walks among the lampstands knows your situation, holds all authority, and promises to be with you always, even to the end of the age.

QUESTIONS FOR REFLECTION

As we pause to consider this magnificent vision of Christ, let's allow His Spirit to search our hearts:

1. Which aspect of Christ's glory most speaks to your heart today—His majesty, His authority, or His tender care?

2. Where do you need to hear Jesus say "Fear not" in your life right now?

3. How will seeing Jesus in His full glory change the way you worship and serve this week?

4. In what ways have you been treating Jesus too casually rather than with reverent awe?

5. When you face hardship or exile like John did, how can you still be "in the Spirit" and continue to worship?

PRAYER RESPONSE

Lord Jesus,

You are far more glorious than we imagined. Thank You for showing us Your majesty while still reaching out to touch us with tender care. Help us live today as those who have truly seen You.

Give us courage when we're afraid, strength when we're weak, and hope when we're discouraged. May we never forget that You walk among us.

In Your mighty name, Amen.

VICTORY DECLARATION

Because of who Christ is, as revealed in Revelation 1, we stand and declare:

- Christ reigns in glory over all creation.
- His power remains unmatched and unchanging.
- His care for us is personal and perpetual.
- His victory is certain and complete.
- Death itself is subject to His authority.

Therefore, we will walk in confidence, not fear, knowing that the One who holds the keys of Death and Hades holds us in His right hand.

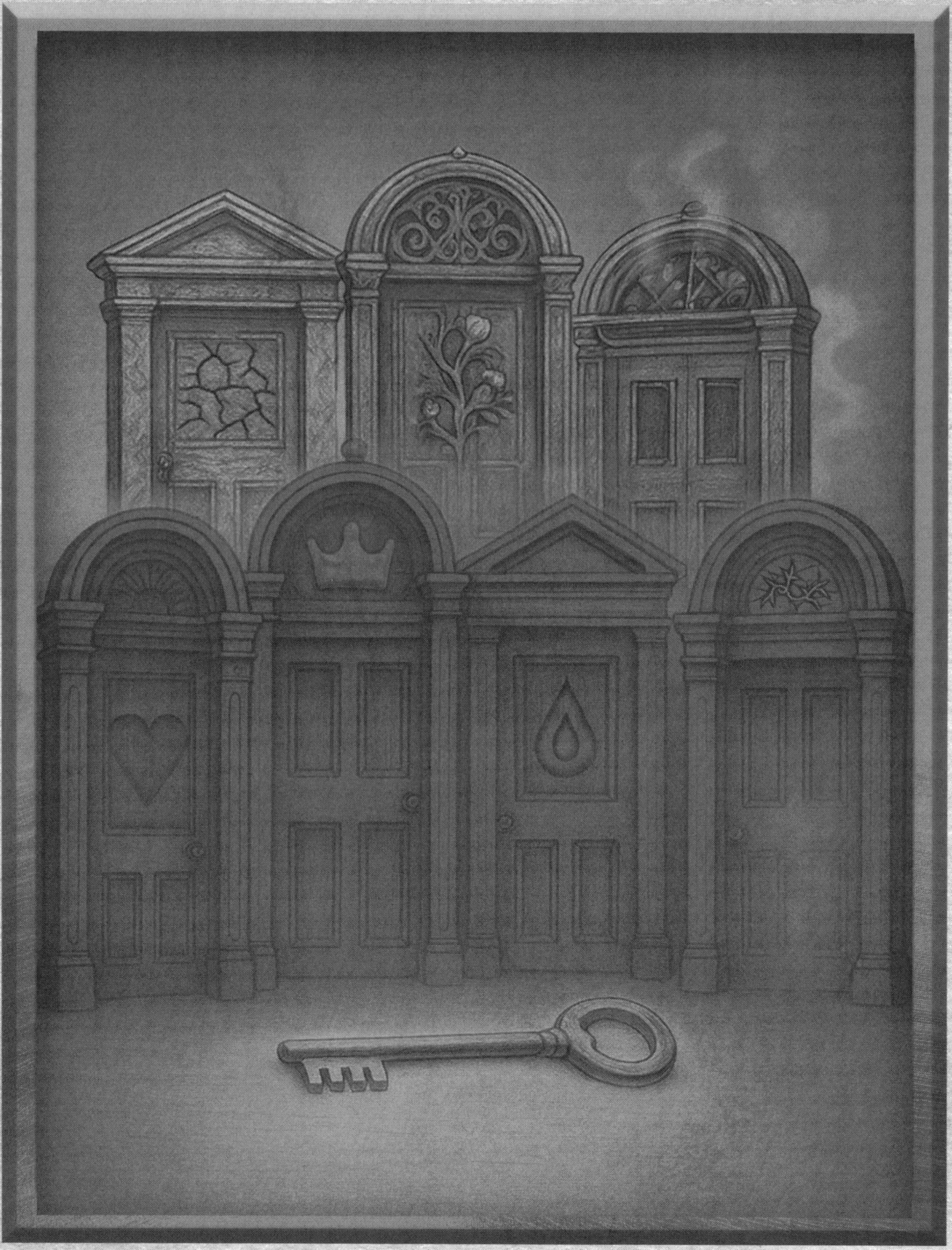

PART TWO

LETTERS TO GOD'S PEOPLE (REVELATION 2-3)

Begin by reading Revelation 2:1-3:22

Making It Personal

Have you ever received a personal letter that changed your life? Perhaps it offered much-needed encouragement during a difficult time or delivered a loving but firm correction that set you on a better path. The seven letters in Revelation 2–3 are exactly this kind of correspondence—deeply personal, remarkably specific, and potentially life-changing. Though written to ancient churches, they speak with startling relevance to our situations today.

Understanding Christ's Heart for His Churches

When Jesus speaks to His churches, He speaks with intimate knowledge and deep concern. Think about this for a moment: the same glorious Christ we saw in chapter one—the One whose face shines like the sun—now bends down to address the specific situations of local churches. What tenderness! What care!

The messages come from Jesus who holds the seven stars in His right hand and walks among the seven golden lampstands. These aren't just beautiful images; they reveal profound truth about Christ's relationship with His church. The stars represent church leaders, whom Christ holds in His powerful yet tender hand. The lampstands are the churches themselves, among which Christ continually walks. He knows our struggles. He sees our faithfulness. He understands our challenges.

You might wonder why Jesus addressed only seven churches when there were certainly more in Asia Minor at the time. The number seven in Scripture represents completeness or perfection. These seven historical churches paint a portrait of church life throughout all generations. Their struggles are our struggles. Their victories can be our victories.

HISTORICAL BACKGROUND: The Seven Cities

These seven cities formed a natural mail route in ancient Asia Minor (modern Turkey). A messenger would travel from Ephesus north to Smyrna and Pergamum, then southeast to Thyatira, Sardis, Philadelphia, and finally Laodicea. Each city had distinct characteristics:

- **Ephesus**–A major port city and commercial center, home to the temple of Artemis.
- **Smyrna**–A beautiful port city known for its loyalty to Rome.
- **Pergamum**–Famous for its library and medical center, with a prominent hill featuring pagan temples.
- **Thyatira**–Known for textile production and trade guilds requiring participation in pagan rituals.
- **Sardis**–An ancient wealthy capital known for its impregnable citadel (that had been captured twice by surprise).
- **Philadelphia**–A smaller city that served as a missionary outpost.
- **Laodicea**–A wealthy banking center known for eye salve, textile industry, and lukewarm water supply.

THE DIVINE PATTERN

Each message flows from Christ's pastoral heart in a beautiful pattern:

1. Each letter begins with "To the angel of the church in [city name], write…"
2. Jesus introduces Himself using imagery from chapter 1 particularly relevant to that church's situation.
3. He commends what He can (except in Laodicea's case, where no commendation was possible).
4. He points out what needs correction (except in Smyrna and Philadelphia, where His words are entirely encouraging).
5. He calls for specific responses, usually including repentance.
6. He promises rewards to those who overcome.
7. Each letter ends with, "Whoever has ears, let them hear what the Spirit says to the churches."

This pattern reveals Christ's pastoral approach: He affirms before correcting, diagnoses accurately, prescribes specifically, and always holds out hope and promises to those who respond.

THE LOVELESS CHURCH (EPHESUS)

The church at Ephesus looked impressive on paper. They worked hard, showed remarkable patience, and maintained doctrinal purity. They tested those who claimed apostolic authority and refused to tolerate evil. By all outward appearances, they were a model church.

But something vital was missing—their first love. They had truth without tenderness, orthodoxy without passion. The flame of love that once burned bright had dimmed to mere embers. It's a sobering reminder that we can do all the right things for all the wrong reasons.

Jesus' prescription cuts to the heart: Remember where you have fallen. Repent of your loveless orthodoxy. Return to those first works. What were those "first works"? The very same activities they were doing now, but originally motivated by love rather than duty. The warning comes with gravity: without love, even right actions lose their value in God's eyes. A church without love isn't really a church at all.

CROSS REFERENCE: Love as Foundation

Jesus' rebuke to Ephesus echoes His teaching in Matthew 22:37–40, where He identifies love for God and neighbor as the foundation of all obedience. It also parallels Paul's famous words in 1 Corinthians 13:1–3 (NIV, 2011): "If I speak in the tongues of men or of angels, but do not have love, I am only a resounding gong or a clanging cymbal... If I give all I possess to the poor and give over my body to hardship that I may boast, but do not have love, I gain nothing."

THE PERSECUTED CHURCH (SMYRNA)

Smyrna offers a striking contrast to Ephesus. While this church received no criticism, they also received no comfort—only the call to endure suffering faithfully. Jesus acknowledges their poverty while declaring them spiritually rich, and He warns of coming persecution.

The believers in Smyrna would face imprisonment and testing for "ten days"—likely symbolizing a defined but limited period of intense suffering. Jesus' exhortation is simple but profound: "Be faithful, even to the point of death, and I will give you the crown of life."

This church reminds us that spiritual prosperity often comes with material poverty, and faithfulness sometimes costs everything. We have many brothers and sisters in churches around the world today who are experiencing the reality Smyrna faced. The question for us is: How will we respond when our faith is tested by fire?

THE COMPROMISED CHURCH (PERGAMUM)

Pergamum represents the compromised church. They were commended for being faithful despite "Satan's throne" being in their city—likely a reference to the prominent altar to Zeus, the medical cult of Asclepius (whose symbol was a serpent), and the center of emperor worship. This church maintained faithful witness even when Antipas, Christ's faithful witness, was put to death among them.

Yet they tolerated those who held to the "teaching of Balaam" and the "Nicolaitans." These false teachings led to two primary sins: eating food sacrificed to idols and sexual immorality. Both were likely connected to the social pressure to participate in pagan worship, which often involved ritual meals and sexual practices. By compromising in these areas, believers could avoid economic hardship and social ostracism.

Jesus warns this church that unless they repent, He will "come to you soon and will fight against them with the sword of my mouth." The reference to the sword recalls the vision in chapter 1 where a sharp, double-edged sword comes from Christ's mouth. This sword symbolizes the Word of God that judges and divides truth from error, exposing compromise.

The lesson for us is clear: We cannot serve both Christ and culture when they demand opposing allegiances. Every generation faces its own versions of "food sacrificed to idols" and "sexual immorality"—areas where cultural acceptance requires spiritual compromise.

WORD STUDY: Balaam

The reference to "Balaam" recalls the Old Testament figure who, unable to curse Israel directly, advised Balak to entice Israel into idolatry and sexual immorality (Numbers 22–25; 31:16). This resulted in God's judgment against Israel. By invoking Balaam, Jesus warns that spiritual compromise often begins with seemingly small accommodations to pagan culture but leads to serious consequences. The Nicolaitans appear to have taught similar compromises, possibly promoting the idea that Christians could participate in pagan practices without spiritual harm.

THE CORRUPTED CHURCH (THYATIRA)

The church at Thyatira received commendation for their love, faith, service, and patient endurance—even growing in these virtues over time. Yet they tolerated a false prophetess symbolically called "Jezebel," who led believers into sexual immorality and idolatry.

The historical Jezebel (1 Kings 16–21) was a foreign queen who brought Baal worship into Israel and persecuted God's prophets. This "Jezebel" in Thyatira likewise introduced corrupt teachings that blended Christian faith with pagan practices.

Jesus' response is severe, promising judgment for this false teacher and her followers while encouraging those who have "not learned Satan's so-called deep secrets" to hold fast to what they have.

THE DEAD CHURCH (SARDIS)

Sardis presents a sobering warning: It's possible to have a reputation for being alive while being spiritually dead. Like their city, which had fallen twice to enemies due to overconfidence, the church had grown complacent. They had a name, a reputation, even programs and activities—but no spiritual vitality.

Jesus' prescription is urgent: "Wake up! Strengthen what remains and is about to die." Their works were incomplete, their faith was shallow, and their security was false. They needed to remember what they had received, obey it, and repent.

Yet even in this "dead" church, some had "not soiled their clothes"—a faithful remnant who maintained their spiritual integrity. Jesus promises that these faithful ones will walk with Him in white, symbolic of purity and victory.

THE FAITHFUL CHURCH (PHILADELPHIA)

Like Smyrna, Philadelphia received no rebuke, only encouragement. Though they had "little strength," they had kept Christ's word and not denied His name. Despite opposition from those who claimed to be God's people but were not, this church remained faithful.

Jesus promises to open doors that no one can shut—opportunities for ministry and witness that their opponents cannot block. He will make their persecutors acknowledge God's love for them and will protect them from the "hour of trial" coming on the world.

The reward for this church includes becoming pillars in God's temple and receiving new names—imagery suggesting permanent place, importance, and transformed identity in God's presence.

THE LUKEWARM CHURCH (LAODICEA)

The final church receives the harshest rebuke and no commendation whatsoever: "I know your deeds, that you are neither cold nor hot. I wish you were either one or the other! So, because you are lukewarm—neither hot nor cold—I am about to spit you out of my mouth."

This rebuke had special significance for Laodicea, which received its water through an aqueduct. To the north, Hierapolis had hot springs that were therapeutic and healing. To the east, Colossae had refreshingly cold mountain water. But by the time water reached Laodicea through its aqueduct system, it was neither refreshingly cold nor therapeutically hot—just lukewarm and mineral-laden, causing nausea. Their spiritual condition produced the same effect in Christ.

Many take the word "cold" as negative and "hot" as positive. But both "cold" and "hot" should be taken as positive, while "lukewarm" is negative. The lukewarm, half-committed, apathetic person turns God's stomach such that He will spit them out of His mouth.

The core problem was self-deception: "You say, 'I am rich; I have acquired wealth and do not need a thing.' But you do not realize that you are wretched, pitiful, poor, blind and naked." Material prosperity had blinded them to spiritual poverty. They felt self-sufficient, but in reality, they were spiritually bankrupt.

Yet even to this church, Jesus extends hope and invitation: "Here I am! I stand at the door and knock." This isn't primarily an evangelistic appeal to unbelievers but a call to a church that had excluded Christ from its life. The Lord desires renewed fellowship with His wayward people. Jesus stands outside, knocking to come in.

HISTORICAL BACKGROUND: Laodicea's Prosperity

Laodicea was known for three primary industries that Jesus references in His rebuke:

1. **Banking and wealth**—The city was so wealthy that when destroyed by an earthquake in AD 60, they rebuilt without Roman aid.
2. **Textile industry**—Famous for black wool clothing and fabric.
3. 3**Medical school**—Renowned for producing "Phrygian powder," an eye salve.

Jesus offers true spiritual gold, white garments, and eye salve—divine solutions that directly address their physical sources of pride.

THE SPIRIT SPEAKS

The Spirit speaks to the church, so the church must listen! Each letter concludes with the exhortation: "Whoever has ears, let them hear what the Spirit says to the churches." Notice the plural "churches"—every message, though addressed to a specific congregation, applies to all churches throughout history.

These seven churches represent the complete spectrum of church life in every generation. We can find elements of each church in our own congregations and even in our individual spiritual lives.

All churches are not the same, so we must ask: Is what the Spirit says about these churches true of our church, whether bad or good? Is it true about you? Which church most resembles your spiritual condition today?

He who has an ear, let him hear what the Spirit says to the churches.

QUESTIONS FOR REFLECTION

Take a moment to let the Spirit search your heart as you consider:

1. In which of these churches do you see your own spiritual condition reflected? Perhaps you share Ephesus's doctrinal precision but need to rekindle love's flame. Maybe you identify with Sardis's outward success hiding inner emptiness. Or do you recognize Laodicea's comfortable self-sufficiency in your own heart?

2. What areas of compromise have slowly crept into your life? Where have you grown content with lukewarm devotion?

3. What would Jesus commend in your current walk with Him, and what would He ask you to change?

4. How do the promises to those who overcome motivate you to remain faithful?

PRAYER RESPONSE

Lord Jesus,

You who walk among Your churches, examine our hearts today. Where love has grown cold, breathe Your warmth back into our souls. Where compromise has subtly entered, grant us courage to stand firm. Where self-sufficiency has taken root, teach us again our deep need for You.

Thank You for Your patient correction and faithful promises. Help us truly hear what Your Spirit is saying to us today.

In Your holy name, Amen.

VICTORY DECLARATION

We stand confident today in powerful truths: Christ still walks among His churches, seeing all and caring deeply. His love pursues us even when we wander. His grace offers new beginnings to all who repent. His promises remain sure to those who overcome.

Therefore, we move forward with renewed purpose, holding fast to what we have received, knowing that the One who calls us is faithful, and He will surely complete His work in us.

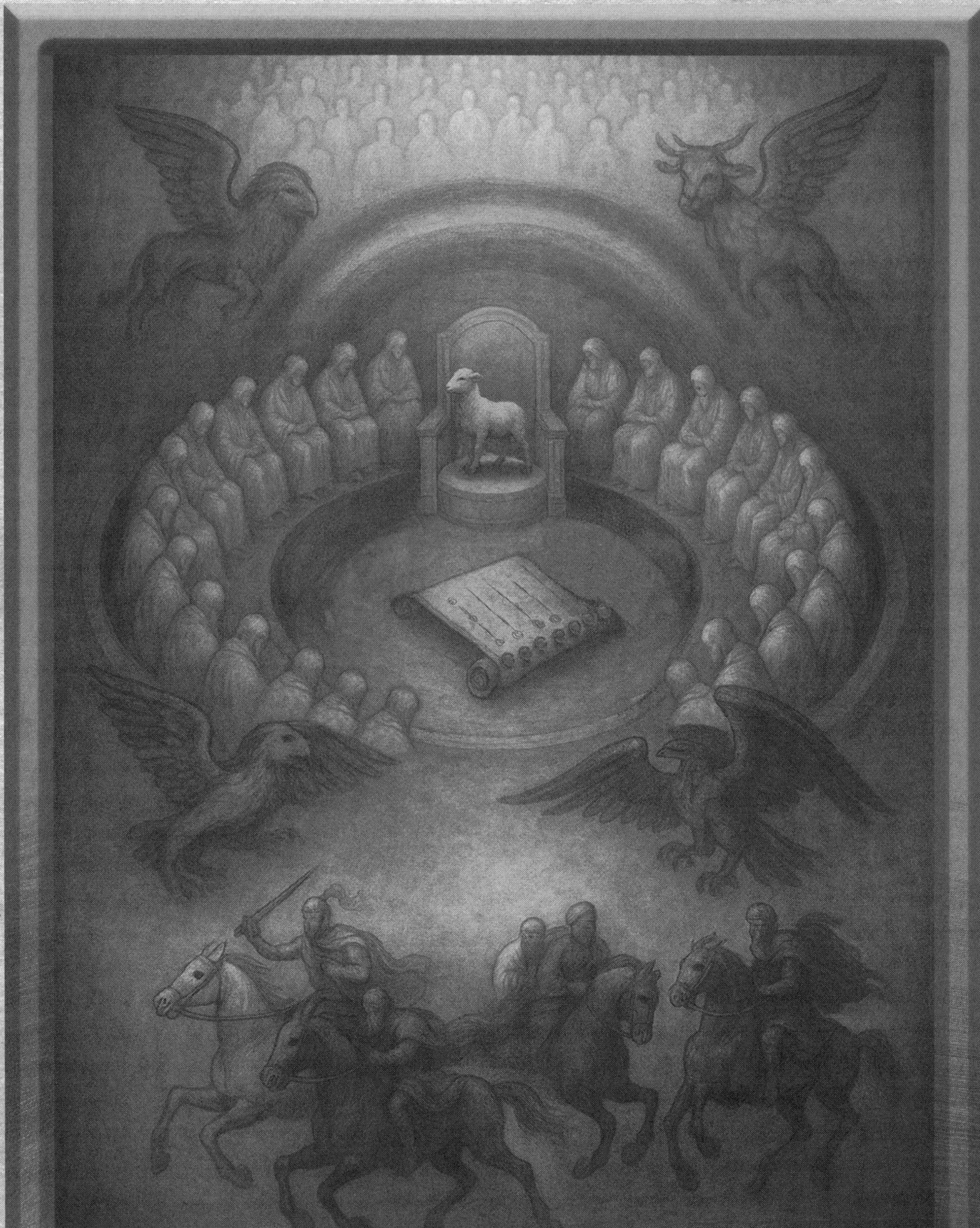

PART THREE

HEAVEN'S PERSPECTIVE (REVELATION 4-7)

Begin by reading Revelation 4:1-5:14

Making It Personal

"Pay no attention to the man behind the curtain!" That famous line from "The Wizard of Oz" reveals the deception behind human power. Like the Wizard's intimidating projection, worldly powers want us to focus on their apparent strength while ignoring the reality behind the scenes. But what if we could see beyond the veil of this world to ultimate reality? What if we could glimpse who truly rules the universe?

The Throne Room Vision

"After this I looked, and behold, a door standing open in heaven!" With these words, John invites us to see what few human eyes have ever witnessed—the very throne room of God. The scene shifts dramatically from earth to heaven, from the struggling churches to the sovereign center of all creation.

John pulls back the curtain to reveal who truly reigns. In the midst of Roman persecution, with Caesar demanding worship and the empire flexing its military might, this vision answers the most important question: Who is really in charge? When your world seems chaotic, when evil appears to be winning, when suffering touches your life—this throne room vision provides the ultimate comfort.

THE GLORY OF THE ONE ON THE THRONE

As John's eyes adjust to the heavenly scene, he sees a throne. Not Caesar's throne, not a throne of human power, but THE throne—the seat of all true authority in the universe. And Someone sits on that throne.

John struggles to describe the indescribable. The One on the throne has the appearance of jasper and carnelian, precious stones that likely represent God's holiness, majesty, and judgment. A rainbow, resembling an emerald, encircles the throne, reminding us of God's covenant faithfulness even amid judgment.

Around this central throne sit twenty-four elders on twenty-four thrones, clothed in white garments with golden crowns on their heads. Who are these elders? Most likely they represent all of God's redeemed people—the twelve tribes of Israel from the Old Testament and the twelve apostles from the New Testament. Together, they symbolize the completeness of God's people throughout all ages.

From the throne come flashes of lightning, rumblings, and peals of thunder—signs of God's awesome power and presence. Before the throne burn seven torches of fire, which are the seven spirits of God—the Holy Spirit in His perfect work.

WORD STUDY: Sea of Glass

The "sea of glass, clear as crystal" before God's throne has profound significance. In ancient Jewish thought, the sea represented chaos, the untamable forces that threatened human existence. The Israelites feared the sea as a place of danger and uncertainty. Yet here, before God's throne, even the chaos is transformed into perfect stillness—a sea of glass.

When we feel overwhelmed by life's storms, this image reminds us that from heaven's perspective, all chaos is under God's sovereign control. What fears keep you awake at night? What chaos threatens to overwhelm you? Before the throne of God, all chaos becomes a sea of glass—perfectly still, completely contained.

THE LIVING CREATURES AND THEIR WORSHIP

Around the throne stand four living creatures, covered with eyes in front and behind. These mysterious beings resemble the seraphim from Isaiah 6 and the cherubim from Ezekiel 1. The first creature resembles a lion, the second an ox, the third has a face like a human, and the fourth resembles an eagle in flight.

CROSS REFERENCE: Heavenly Beings

The four living creatures echo similar visions in the Old Testament:

- **Isaiah 6:2–3 (ESV)**—"Above him stood the seraphim. Each had six wings… And one called to another and said: 'Holy, holy, holy is the LORD of hosts; the whole earth is full of his glory!'"
- **Ezekiel 1:10 (ESV)**—"As for the likeness of their faces, each had a human face. The four had the face of a lion on the right side, the four had the face of an ox on the left side, and the four had the face of an eagle."

These parallels confirm the continuity between Old Testament prophecy and New Testament revelation. The same God who spoke through Isaiah and Ezekiel now speaks through John.

These creatures likely represent the best of God's created order—the majesty of the lion, the strength of the ox, the intelligence of humanity, and the swiftness of the eagle. Together, they proclaim the holiness of God day and night without ceasing: "Holy, holy, holy is the Lord God Almighty, who was and is and is to come!"

Notice they don't say "loving, loving, loving," though God certainly is love. They don't say "merciful, merciful, merciful," though His mercy endures forever. They proclaim His holiness—His absolute moral perfection and His complete otherness. He is wholly different from everything else in existence. There is no one like our God!

When the living creatures give glory and honor and thanks to the One seated on the throne, the twenty-four elders fall down in worship. They cast their crowns before the throne, declaring, "Worthy are you, our Lord and God, to receive glory and honor and power, for you created all things, and by your will they existed and were created."

This is ultimate reality—all of creation exists for God's glory, and all redeemed humanity finds its highest purpose in worshiping Him. The elders cast their crowns before Him, recognizing that any honor they've received is ultimately from Him and belongs to Him.

THE SCROLL AND THE LAMB

As chapter 5 opens, John notices something in the right hand of the One seated on the throne—a scroll written within and on the back, sealed with seven seals. This scroll likely contains God's purposes for history and creation, the unfolding of His sovereign plan. But there's a problem: no one in heaven or on earth or under the earth can open the scroll.

John begins to weep loudly. Why such intense emotion? Because if no one can open the scroll, then God's purposes remain unfulfilled. If no one is worthy to reveal and implement God's plan, then evil may continue unchecked. John's tears reflect the longing of all creation for redemption and justice.

But then one of the elders says, "Weep no more; behold, the Lion of the tribe of Judah, the Root of David, has conquered, so that he can open the scroll and its seven seals."

HISTORICAL BACKGROUND: Ancient Scrolls

In ancient times, important documents were written on scrolls made of papyrus or parchment. Legal documents, particularly wills or property deeds, were sealed with multiple seals to prevent tampering and unauthorized access. Only someone with proper authority could break the seals.

The scroll in Revelation 5 appears to be a title deed to the earth or the document containing God's redemptive plan for creation. The seven seals suggest it is the most secure document possible, containing God's perfect and complete purposes. That only the Lamb can open it emphasizes Christ's unique authority to execute God's plan for history and redemption.

THE LION WHO IS A LAMB

John turns, expecting to see a mighty lion, but instead sees "a Lamb standing, as though it had been slain." This paradox captures the heart of the gospel—the conquering Lion is also the sacrificed Lamb. The way Jesus conquered was not through military might, but through sacrificial death.

This Lamb has seven horns, symbolizing complete power, and seven eyes, representing perfect knowledge through the seven spirits of God. Jesus is omnipotent, omniscient, and through the Holy Spirit, omnipresent. Nothing escapes His notice; nothing exceeds His ability.

When the Lamb takes the scroll, worship erupts again. The living creatures and elders fall down before the Lamb with harps and golden bowls full of incense, which are the prayers of the saints. They sing a new song: "Worthy are you to take the scroll and to open its seals, for you were slain, and by your blood you ransomed people for God from every tribe and language and people and nation."

WORD STUDY: Ransom

The Greek word translated "ransomed" (agorazō) means "to purchase" or "to buy out of the marketplace." In ancient times, a person could purchase a slave from the marketplace to set them free. This is precisely what Christ has done for us.

The idea of ransom indicates that:

- A price was paid (Christ's blood)
- People were in bondage (to sin and death)
- Liberation was the goal
- Ownership transferred (from darkness to God's kingdom)

As the song declares, "by your blood you ransomed people for God"—emphasizing that the purpose of our redemption is not merely our freedom but our belonging to God.

Why is Jesus worthy? Because He was slain as our substitute. By His blood, Jesus ransomed people for God. The idea of ransom is that a price is paid to free someone. No amount of money can save a sinner—only the precious blood of Christ!

And notice who Jesus has ransomed—people from every tribe, language, people, and nation. Jesus has died for every people group in the world. He is not just one race's Savior; He is the Savior of any and all who call upon Him. This is why the church is called to make disciples of all nations. The gospel is for everyone!

HEAVEN'S SONG

The worship intensifies as countless angels join in, saying with a loud voice, "Worthy is the Lamb who was slain, to receive power and wealth and wisdom and might and honor and glory and blessing!"

The word "worthy" means to ascribe weight or worth to something. Jesus is weighty! He's not thin like tin foil! He has substance! Jesus is worthy of all attention, all glory, all praise, and all honor in heaven and earth. He is the only object truly deserving of worship.

But what if you don't feel like worshiping Jesus? As Pastor J.D. Greear wisely observed, "The central premise in worship is not what you feel like, but what God is worthy of." You worship based on who God is and what He has promised, not on your feelings. Worship is putting the worthiness of God on display.

The question for us to ponder is this: Is Jesus at the center of our worship? Yes, Jesus is sitting on the throne of heaven, but is He seated on the throne of our lives? Or are we trying to sit on the throne and ask Jesus to take a side chair?

WORSHIPING IN SPIRIT AND TRUTH

When we understand the heavenly throne room, our worship on earth changes. No longer are we merely singing songs or performing religious rituals—we are joining a cosmic symphony that has been ongoing since before time began and will continue throughout eternity. The worship of heaven becomes the pattern for our worship on earth.

Several principles emerge from heaven's throne room that should guide our worship:

1. **God-Centered Focus:** All attention in heaven is on the One seated on the throne and the Lamb. Our worship must be theocentric, not anthropocentric. We don't worship primarily for what we get out of it, but because God is worthy.

2. **Holiness Recognition:** The living creatures continually proclaim God's holiness. When we grasp God's utter perfection and complete otherness, casual or flippant approaches to worship become unthinkable.

3. **Costly Surrender:** The twenty-four elders cast their crowns before the throne. True worship involves surrender—giving back to God what He has given us and acknowledging His rightful ownership of all.

4. **Cross Centrality:** The Lamb who was slain stands at the center of heaven's worship. Our worship must always revolve around the cross and resurrection of Jesus Christ.

5. **Diverse Unity:** People from every tribe, language, people, and nation join together in unified worship. Our worship should reflect this diverse unity, embracing various cultural expressions while maintaining doctrinal fidelity.

When we worship with these principles in mind, our earthly gatherings become a rehearsal for eternity. We join our voices with those of angels, living creatures, and saints from every age. We step out of time and into the eternal reality of God's presence. Even our most sublime moments of worship here are merely a foretaste of what awaits us.

QUESTIONS FOR REFLECTION

1. How does seeing the throne room of heaven change your perspective on the challenges you're facing today?

2. In what ways have you cast your "crown" before Jesus, acknowledging that all you have belongs to Him?

3. What areas of your life still need to be surrendered to the Lamb who is worthy of all worship?

4. How will this vision of heaven's worship influence your participation in corporate worship this week?

PRAYER RESPONSE

Worthy Lamb of God,

We stand amazed at Your glory and humbled by Your sacrifice. You alone could open the scroll. You alone have ransomed us by Your blood. You alone deserve all worship, honor, and praise.

Forgive us for the times we've placed ourselves or others on the throne that belongs only to You. Help us to live today with heaven's perspective, remembering that You are in control even when our world seems chaotic.

May our lives echo the worship of heaven, declaring Your worth to everyone we meet.

In the name of the Lion who is the Lamb, Amen.

VICTORY DECLARATION

We stand confident today knowing that:

- Our God reigns upon the throne of heaven.
- The Lion of Judah has conquered through sacrifice.
- Jesus has ransomed people from every nation.
- No power in heaven or earth can thwart God's purposes.
- The Lamb is worthy of all worship and honor.

Therefore, we join our voices with the elders, the living creatures, and the countless angels, declaring: "Worthy is the Lamb who was slain!"

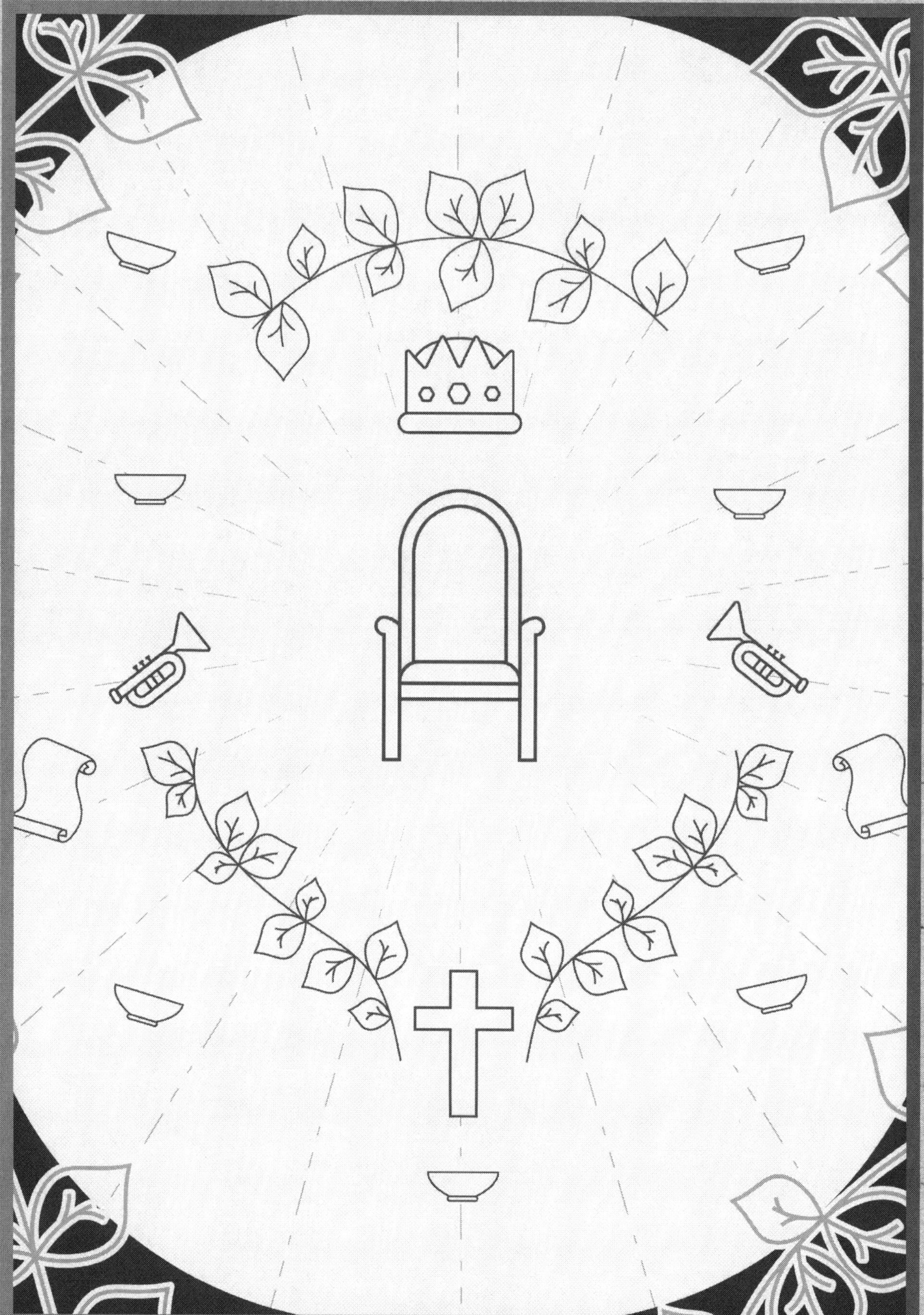

THE SEVEN SEALS (REVELATION 6-8:1)

Begin by reading Revelation 6:1-8:1

Making It Personal

Have you ever looked at the headlines and wondered if the world is spinning out of control? Wars, famines, economic crises, natural disasters—it can seem like chaos reigns. Where is God in all this? The seven seals give us heaven's perspective on earth's troubles. They remind us that even when it appears evil is winning, God remains sovereign, and His purposes will prevail.

Interpreting God's Judgment

As we move from the worship in heaven to the unfolding of divine judgment, we enter some of the most challenging passages in Revelation. The Lamb begins to open the seven seals of the scroll, releasing a series of judgments upon the earth. How are we to understand these dramatic scenes?

Before we examine each seal, let's consider how to approach these judgments. In chapters 6–19, we encounter three sets of seven divine judgments: the seven seals, seven trumpets, and seven bowls. Some read these judgments as occurring in strict chronological sequence. However, if we look carefully, we notice that each set concludes with the final judgment and Christ's return. Rather than consecutive periods, these judgments likely represent the same events told from different angles, with increasing intensity.

TEACHING BOX: Three Sets of Seven Judgments

The Idealist view interprets the three sets of judgments (seals, trumpets, bowls) as different angles on the same events, like watching replays of a football game from different camera positions:

Seven Seals: Basic overview of history's patterns

- Seals 1–5: Ongoing realities throughout history (war, conflict, economic oppression, death, martyrdom)
- Seal 6: The end of history and Day of the Lord.
- Seal 7: Final judgment and what lies beyond.

Seven Trumpets: More detailed view with increased intensity

- Emphasizes God's warnings to repent.
- Partial judgments (typically affecting "one-third")

Seven Bowls: Final, most intense view

- Complete judgments ("It is done!")
- No more opportunity for repentance.

Each series follows the pattern: First four relate to physical/natural world, fifth relates to people's suffering, sixth brings final conflict, seventh brings conclusion.

Think of it like watching a sports replay from multiple camera positions. The first angle shows the basic action, while subsequent angles reveal more details. Similarly, the seals provide the overview, while the trumpets and bowls add increasing detail about God's judgment.

If we embrace an idealist interpretation (which we're using in this study), the first five seals represent ongoing realities throughout history, the sixth seal depicts what happens at history's end, and the seventh seal represents the final judgment and what lies beyond. These judgments remind us that God sees the evil in our world and will ultimately bring justice.

THE FOUR HORSEMEN OF THE APOCALYPSE

As the Lamb opens the first four seals, four horsemen emerge. These iconic figures have captured the imagination of artists and writers for centuries, but what do they represent?

The first horseman rides a white horse. He carries a bow, receives a crown, and goes out conquering. Some mistakenly identify him as Christ because Jesus also rides a white horse in Revelation 19. However, this rider appears as a counterfeit Christ, representing deceptive conquest. Throughout history, various powers have emerged claiming to bring peace while actually bringing oppression. This horseman symbolizes the external conflict of war and conquest.

The second horseman rides a red horse and takes peace from the earth. This rider represents civil conflict—the internal strife that tears nations apart. Think of the civil wars, revolutions, and violent unrest that have marked human history. When peace is taken from the earth, neighbors turn against neighbors, and societies fracture from within.

The third horseman rides a black horse and carries scales. He announces inflated prices for basic necessities while luxury items remain untouched. This rider symbolizes economic oppression and famine—not the kind that affects everyone equally, but the kind that crushes the poor while the wealthy barely notice. We see this pattern repeatedly throughout history: economic systems that create deep inequality.

The fourth horseman rides a pale or ashen horse. His name is Death, and Hades follows him. He has authority to kill with sword, famine, pestilence, and wild beasts. This horseman represents the large-scale death that follows in the wake of war, civil strife, and economic collapse.

> **CROSS REFERENCE: The Four Horsemen and Jesus' Olivet Discourse**
>
> The four horsemen closely parallel Jesus' warnings about the end times in Matthew 24:
>
> - First Horseman (Conquest) → "Many will come in my name... and will lead many astray." (Matthew 24:5)
> - Second Horseman (War) → "You will hear of wars and rumors of wars ... nation will rise against nation." (Matthew 24:6–7)
> - Third Horseman (Famine) → "There will be famines." (Matthew 24:7)
> - Fourth Horseman (Death) → "And pestilences ... All these are but the beginning of the birth pains." (Matthew 24:7–8)
>
> This connection confirms that these are not just future events but ongoing realities throughout the church age, exactly as Jesus foretold.

Together, these four horsemen remind us that because of humanity's fallen nature, every age is characterized by conquest, conflict, economic injustice, and death. Jesus Himself warned of these very things in Matthew 24. The sobering reality is that these horsemen will continue to ride until Christ returns. Human efforts to create utopia will ultimately fail because the problem lies within the human heart itself. Our only hope is found in Christ.

THE CRY OF THE MARTYRS

When the fifth seal is opened, John sees under the altar the souls of those who had been slain for God's Word and their testimony. These martyrs cry out, "O Sovereign Lord, holy and true, how long before you will judge and avenge our blood on those who dwell on the earth?"

This poignant scene reminds us that throughout history, countless believers have suffered and died for their faith. Even now, in many parts of the world, Christians face intense persecution. The martyrs' cry shows us that it's appropriate to long for God's justice. They don't seek personal revenge but divine justice.

God gives each martyr a white robe, symbolizing purity, righteousness, and vindication. Though the world rejected them, God receives them. Though earthly courts condemned them, the Supreme Court of heaven overturns that verdict. But they must wait a little longer until the full number of their fellow servants should be killed. This sobering statement reminds us that Christian suffering isn't over—more martyrs will join their ranks before Christ returns.

HISTORICAL BACKGROUND: Persecution in John's Day

The first-century church faced various forms of persecution:

- **Social ostracism:** Christians were often excluded from trade guilds and normal social functions because these typically involved pagan religious rituals.
- **Economic hardship:** Without participation in local trade guilds (which required honoring pagan deities), many believers struggled financially.
- **Legal sanctions:** Since Christians refused to participate in emperor worship, they could be charged with treason or impiety.
- **Violent persecution:** While systematic empire-wide persecution came later, local outbreaks occurred. Nero blamed Christians for Rome's fire in 64 AD, leading to torture and execution.

Under Domitian (likely emperor when Revelation was written), emperor worship intensified. Christians who refused to burn incense to Caesar and declare "Caesar is Lord" faced martyrdom—exactly the situation John describes in the fifth seal.

THE DAY OF GOD'S WRATH

The opening of the sixth seal brings cosmic upheaval. The sun becomes black, the moon becomes like blood, the stars fall to earth, the sky vanishes, and every mountain and island

moves from its place. This apocalyptic imagery describes the collapse of the current world order as Christ returns.

When this happens, people from every level of society—kings and generals, rich and poor—hide themselves, crying for the mountains to fall on them. They ask, "Who can stand before the wrath of the Lamb?" It's a haunting question. If even mountains cannot stand before God's judgment, how can sinful humans hope to endure?

This vivid scene draws on Old Testament prophecies about the Day of the Lord, when God intervenes dramatically in human history: The upheaval in the physical cosmos symbolizes the collapse

> **Joel 2:31 (ESV):** "The sun shall be turned to darkness, and the moon to blood, before the great and awesome day of the LORD comes."

> **Isaiah 34:4 (ESV):** "All the host of heaven shall rot away, and the skies roll up like a scroll. All their host shall fall, as leaves fall from the vine, like leaves falling from the fig tree."

of human power structures and false security. Everything people rely on apart from God—political systems, economic strength, military might—will prove inadequate on that day.

The irony is striking: Those who rejected the Lamb now face the Lamb's wrath. The same Jesus who came in humility to save will return in glory to judge. The question "Who can stand?" acknowledges that no one can stand before God's judgment on their own merits.

THE SEALED OF GOD

Before the seventh seal is opened, John sees four angels holding back the four winds of the earth. Another angel cries out, "Do not harm the earth or the sea or the trees, until we have sealed the servants of our God on their foreheads." God's judgment pauses momentarily while His people are protected.

John hears that 144,000 from every tribe of Israel are sealed, but when he looks, he sees a great multitude that no one could number, from every nation, tribe, people, and language. This multitude stands before the throne in white robes, waving palm branches and crying out, "Salvation belongs to our God who sits on the throne, and to the Lamb!"

WORD STUDY: Sealed

The Greek word for "seal" (sphragis) refers to a signet mark that indicates ownership, authenticity, or protection. In ancient times, important documents were sealed with a wax impression from a signet ring to prove their authenticity and to protect them from tampering.

In the Old Testament, Ezekiel 9:4 describes a protective mark placed on the foreheads of the faithful: "Pass through the city, through Jerusalem, and put a mark on the foreheads of the men who sigh and groan over all the abominations that are committed in it." This mark protected them from coming judgment.

When Revelation speaks of believers being "sealed," it indicates that:

1. They belong to God (ownership)
2. They are authentic members of His family (authenticity)
3. They are protected through judgment (protection)

While this seal is not physically visible, it is spiritually real - the Holy Spirit Himself is the seal of God's ownership (Ephesians 1:13–14).

The number 144,000 has led to much confusion. Some groups, like Jehovah's Witnesses, have taken this literally to mean only 144,000 will be saved. But numbers in Revelation are typically symbolic. Twelve represents the completeness of God's people (twelve tribes, twelve apostles), and one thousand symbolizes a vast number. Multiplied together (12 × 12 × 1,000), we get completeness multiplied by completeness multiplied by vastness—in other words, all of God's people throughout history.

John's vision beautifully portrays the fulfillment of God's covenant promises. What began with Israel now includes people from every nation. All together, they worship before the throne, having come out of the great tribulation. Their robes are made white in the blood of the Lamb—a paradoxical image that reminds us that Christ's death cleanses us from all sin.

The promise to this multitude is breathtaking: "They shall hunger no more, neither thirst anymore; the sun shall not strike them, nor any scorching heat... and God will wipe away every tear from their eyes." In the presence of God, all suffering ends. What we endure now is temporary, but our joy in God's presence will be eternal.

THE SEVENTH SEAL

When the Lamb opens the seventh seal, there is silence in heaven for about half an hour. After the thunderous worship and dramatic judgments, this silence feels weighty. It recalls Old Testament passages like Zephaniah 1:7: "Be silent before the Lord GOD! For the day of the LORD is near."

This silence suggests the solemnity of final judgment. When God makes His final judgment, all arguments cease. There are no more excuses, no more appeals, no more chances. The silence also creates suspense, preparing us for the next cycle of judgments through the seven trumpets.

The half-hour duration symbolizes a brief but significant pause. In the presence of Almighty God, even a short silence can feel eternal. Imagine the scene: countless angels, the four living

creatures, the twenty-four elders, and the great multitude—all silent before the awesome majesty of God's final judgment.

HOPE IN TRIBULATION

What does this vision of the seven seals mean for us today? Several truths emerge:

First, we must maintain a wartime mentality. The four horsemen continue to ride. Spiritual warfare continues around us. We cannot afford to grow complacent or comfortable in this world.

Second, we must remember that present sufferings are temporary. Though the martyrs cry "How long?", their white robes remind us that vindication is coming. The tears we shed now will one day be wiped away by God's own hand.

Third, we must recognize that God's judgment is certain. Though it may seem delayed, the day will come when the question "Who can stand?" will be on every lip. Our only hope is to be among those sealed by God, those whose robes are washed white in the blood of the Lamb.

Finally, we must keep our eyes on the glorious future promised to God's people. Whatever tribulation we face now, it cannot compare to the joy of standing before God's throne, hunger and thirst satisfied, every tear wiped away.

QUESTIONS FOR REFLECTION

1. How does understanding the four horsemen as ongoing realities throughout history change your perspective on current events?

2. In what ways might you need to develop more of a "wartime mentality" in your spiritual life?

3. How does the promise that God will wipe away every tear comfort you in your current struggles?

4. Where do you see evidence of the four horsemen at work in our world today?

PRAYER RESPONSE

Sovereign Lord,

You hold history in Your hands. Nothing escapes Your notice—not the aggression of conquerors, not the suffering of the poor, not the tears of the persecuted. Though the horsemen ride and chaos seems to reign, we trust Your perfect timing and Your perfect justice.

Protect us with Your seal as we navigate a world filled with darkness. Help us to live as those who belong to You, keeping our eyes fixed on the day when we will stand before Your throne with that countless multitude from every nation.

Until that day, give us courage to endure, faith to persevere, and love to reach those who don't yet know You. And when we grow weary, remind us that You will wipe away every tear from our eyes.

In the name of the Lamb who was slain, Amen.

VICTORY DECLARATION

We stand confident today knowing that:

- God's people are sealed and protected through tribulation
- The blood of the Lamb makes sinners pure and holy
- A countless multitude from every nation will worship before the throne
- The horsemen ride only within the limits God allows
- The day is coming when God will wipe away every tear

Therefore, we will not fear what man can do to us, for our salvation belongs to our God who sits on the throne, and to the Lamb!

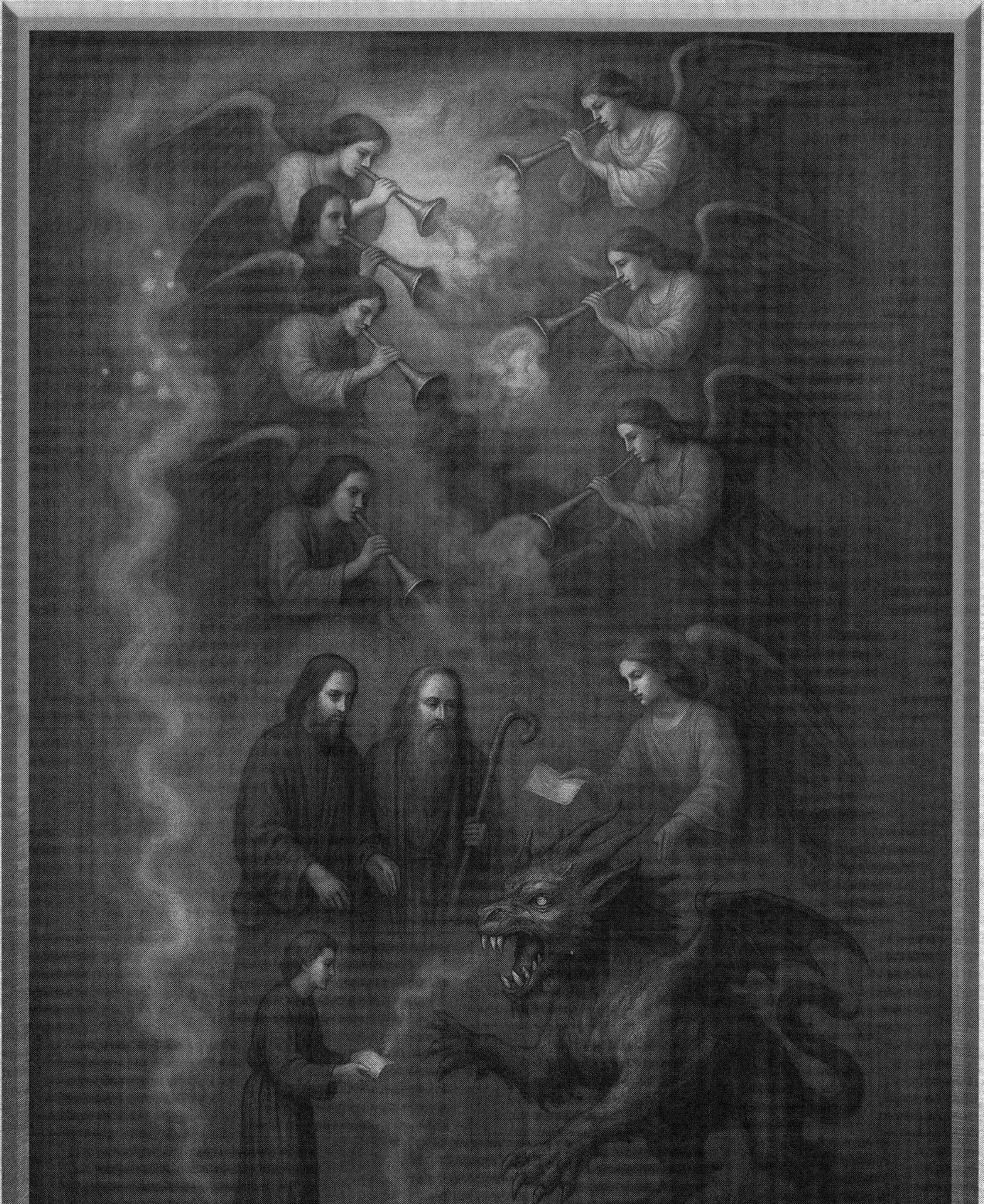

PART FOUR

WARNING TRUMPETS (REVELATION 8-11)

Begin by reading Revelation 8:2-11:19

Making It Personal

Have you ever been awakened by a shrill alarm in the middle of the night? Perhaps it was a smoke detector warning of danger, or maybe a severe weather alert on your phone. While jarring and unwelcome, these warnings serve a vital purpose—they alert us to imminent threats so we can take protective action. The trumpet judgments in Revelation function much like divine alarm systems, warning humanity of the consequences of continued rebellion while offering a window for repentance before final judgment falls.

When Prayer Moves Heaven

As we begin our study of the seven trumpets, we encounter a powerful image that should transform how we pray. An angel takes a golden censer, fills it with incense mixed with "the prayers of all the saints," and offers it on the golden altar before God's throne. Then something remarkable happens: the angel fills the censer with fire from the altar and throws it onto the earth, resulting in "peals of thunder, rumblings, flashes of lightning, and an earthquake."

This vivid picture reveals an astounding truth: our prayers participate in God's activity in the world. The prayers of God's people aren't just heard; they're gathered, mingled with incense (perhaps representing Christ's intercession), and presented before God. These same prayers become instruments of God's judgment on the earth.

When you pray "Your kingdom come, Your will be done," you're not merely uttering pious words. You're participating in the cosmic struggle between good and evil. Your prayers for justice, for the gospel's advancement, for Christ's return—they rise to heaven and return to earth as divine action. Every "Lord, how long?" that ascends from the persecuted church is stored in heaven's censers, waiting to be poured out as judgment.

WORD STUDY: Incense and Prayer

The connection between incense and prayer has deep biblical roots. In the Old Testament tabernacle and temple, the priest would burn incense on the golden altar while the people prayed outside (Luke 1:10). The rising smoke symbolized prayers ascending to God.

Psalm 141:2 explicitly makes this connection: "Let my prayer be counted as incense before you, and the lifting up of my hands as the evening sacrifice."

In Revelation 5:8, the twenty-four elders hold "golden bowls full of incense, which are the prayers of the saints." This imagery teaches us that:

1. Our prayers are precious to God (kept in golden bowls).
2. Our prayers are perpetual before God (the incense continues to rise).
3. Our prayers are powerful (they participate in God's purposes).

When we pray, we're not simply speaking words into the air; we're engaging in a sacred activity that has cosmic significance.

This should revolutionize our prayer lives. We don't pray because it's a religious duty. We pray because God uses our prayers to accomplish His purposes in the world. Prayer isn't just talking to God; it's joining His work.

UNDERSTANDING THE TRUMPETS

Seven angels now prepare to sound seven trumpets. In Scripture, trumpets typically serve three purposes: they announce important events, they warn of impending danger, and they signal military action. All three meanings apply here. These trumpets announce God's judgment, warn the unrepentant, and signal divine warfare against evil.

Unlike the seven seals which affected a quarter of the earth, these trumpets impact a third of their targets. The fraction indicates that these judgments, while severe, are still partial and limited. They're designed not just to punish but to warn, giving people opportunity to repent before the final judgment.

CROSS REFERENCE: Trumpets in Scripture

Trumpets play significant roles throughout the Bible:

- **Exodus 19:16–19:** Trumpets announce God's presence on Mount Sinai.
- **Joshua 6:1–20:** Trumpets signal Israel's military action against Jericho.
- **Joel 2:1:** "Blow a trumpet in Zion; sound an alarm on my holy mountain!"
- **1 Thessalonians 4:16:** "The Lord himself will descend from heaven with a cry of command, with the voice of an archangel, and with the sound of the trumpet of God."

- **1 Corinthians 15:52:** "For the trumpet will sound, and the dead will be raised imperishable, and we shall be changed."

The trumpets in Revelation draw on all these associations: divine presence, military action, alarm, and eschatological significance.

NATURAL AND SUPERNATURAL SIGNS

Let's look at what happens when each trumpet sounds:

The first four trumpets unleash environmental disasters. When the first angel blows his trumpet, hail and fire mixed with blood are thrown to earth, burning up a third of the earth, trees, and grass. The second trumpet triggers what looks like a great mountain burning with fire being thrown into the sea, turning a third of the sea to blood and destroying a third of sea life and ships. The third trumpet causes a great star called Wormwood to fall on a third of rivers and springs, making the waters bitter and deadly. The fourth trumpet strikes a third of the sun, moon, and stars, darkening a third of the day and night.

These disasters impact the land, sea, fresh water, and sky—all the essential life-support systems of our planet. They echo the plagues God sent on Egypt, which demonstrated His power over all creation and exposed the impotence of Egypt's gods. Similarly, these trumpet judgments reveal God's sovereignty over all creation and expose the powerlessness of modern idols like technological progress and human achievement.

We don't need to look to some future time to see these disasters. Throughout history, people have experienced natural calamities, environmental degradation, and cosmic disturbances. C.S. Lewis wisely observed, "God whispers to us in our pleasures, speaks in our conscience, but shouts in our pains: it is His megaphone to rouse a deaf world." The question is whether we're listening.

HISTORICAL BACKGROUND: Wormwood

The third trumpet introduces a star called "Wormwood" that makes the waters bitter. This name has important significance.

Wormwood (Greek: ἄψινθος) is a highly bitter plant that grows in the Middle East. In the Old Testament, wormwood symbolized suffering and divine judgment:

- **Jeremiah 9:15 :** "I will feed this people with wormwood, and give them poisonous water to drink."
- **Lamentations 3:15:** "[The Lord] has filled me with bitterness; he has sated me with wormwood."
- **Amos 5:7:** "[They] turn justice to wormwood and cast down righteousness to the earth."

By naming this judgment "Wormwood," Revelation connects it to God's historical pattern of bringing bitter consequences upon those who turn from Him. The bitterness in the water mirrors the bitterness of rejecting God's love and truth.

GOD'S MERCY IN JUDGMENT

After the first four trumpets, John sees an eagle flying overhead, crying, "Woe, woe, woe to those who dwell on the earth!" This introduces the final three trumpets, which bring even more severe judgments.

The fifth trumpet unleashes what look like locusts from the bottomless pit. But these aren't ordinary locusts—they're demonic beings who torment the unsealed for five months. They look like horses prepared for battle, with human faces, women's hair, lions' teeth, and scorpion tails. Their king is Abaddon or Apollyon, names meaning "destruction" or "destroyer."

These locusts represent the spiritual torment and emptiness that afflict those who reject God. When people believe Satan's lies and practice wickedness, the result is misery and despair. We see this all around us—people pursuing happiness through materialism, sensuality, power, or fame, only to discover that these pursuits leave them empty and tormented.

The sixth trumpet releases four bound angels from the Euphrates River, leading a vast army of 200 million mounted troops. This demonic cavalry kills a third of mankind through plagues of fire, smoke, and sulfur. Yet despite this devastation, the survivors refuse to repent of their idolatry, murders, sorcery, sexual immorality, and thefts.

This reveals a sobering truth about human nature: judgment alone doesn't change hearts. People can experience terrible consequences for their sin yet still refuse to turn to God. This helps explain why God sometimes allows evil to continue—He knows that simply punishing sin doesn't produce genuine repentance.

And yet, in these judgments, we can see God's mercy. He limits the destruction to a third, not total. He allows the locusts to torment but not kill. He gives people opportunity to repent after each trumpet. These partial judgments are God's merciful warnings, His "megaphone" to get the world's attention before the final judgment falls.

THE BITTERSWEET SCROLL

Between the sixth and seventh trumpets, John receives a little scroll from a mighty angel. He's told to eat it, and it tastes sweet in his mouth but turns bitter in his stomach. This symbolizes how God's Word brings both joy and sorrow. The gospel is sweet to proclaim but often brings bitter opposition and rejection.

Every believer can relate to this bittersweet experience. There's joy in knowing and sharing God's truth, but heartache when people reject it. The prophets felt this tension. Jeremiah called God's words "the joy and delight of my heart," yet he was persecuted for proclaiming them. Jesus himself wept over Jerusalem even as He brought the good news of God's kingdom.

If you've ever felt discouraged when sharing your faith, remember John's bittersweet scroll. The sweetness of God's Word is worth the bitterness that sometimes follows when we proclaim it.

THE TWO WITNESSES

John is then introduced to two witnesses clothed in sackcloth who prophesy for 1,260 days (3½ years). They have power to bring drought, turn water to blood, and strike the earth with plagues. Yet after their testimony is complete, the beast from the bottomless pit kills them, and the world celebrates their deaths. After 3½ days, however, they're resurrected and ascend to heaven in a cloud.

INTERPRETIVE PERSPECTIVES: The Two Witnesses

There are several ways to understand the two witnesses:

Literal View: Two specific prophets who will appear in the end times, often identified as Moses and Elijah (because of the miracles they perform) or Elijah and Enoch (because neither experienced death).

Symbolic View: The two witnesses represent the church in its prophetic role. Evidence for this interpretation:

- They are called "lampstands" (11:4), which elsewhere in Revelation symbolize churches (1:20).
- Two witnesses were required for valid testimony under Jewish law (Deut 19:15).
- Their 1,260 days of ministry correspond to the time period the church is protected in the wilderness (12:6).

- Their death and resurrection echo Christ's pattern, which the church follows.

Hybrid View: The two witnesses represent the testimony of the church throughout history but may also have a specific end-time fulfillment in two individuals.

In the idealist view we're using, the two witnesses primarily symbolize the church's prophetic ministry throughout the church age.

Who are these witnesses? Some interpret them as two literal prophets (perhaps Elijah and Moses, or Elijah and Enoch). But since the witnesses are called lampstands, and we know from Revelation 1 that lampstands represent churches, they likely symbolize the church in its prophetic role. The two witnesses represent God's people bearing testimony to the truth, even in the face of hostility.

Their story mirrors the gospel narrative. Like Christ, they prophesy and perform miracles. Like Christ, they're killed by their enemies. Like Christ, they rise again and ascend to heaven. And like Christ's death and resurrection, their vindication leads many to give glory to God.

This pattern reminds us that the church follows in Christ's footsteps. We bear witness to the truth. We may suffer for that witness. But ultimately, God vindicates His people. Even when the church appears defeated, God raises it to new life.

RESPONDING TO WARNINGS

When the seventh trumpet sounds, loud voices in heaven declare, "The kingdom of the world has become the kingdom of our Lord and of his Christ, and he shall reign forever and ever." The twenty-four elders fall on their faces in worship, giving thanks that God has begun to reign, that the time for judgment has come, and that the time for rewarding God's servants has arrived.

The final trumpet announces Christ's return and the establishment of His eternal kingdom. All human kingdoms, with their rebellion against God, will be overthrown. Christ will reign supreme, bringing judgment to the destroyers of the earth and rewards to His faithful servants.

This vision reminds us that history is moving toward a definite conclusion. Despite appearances to the contrary, God's kingdom will triumph over all human kingdoms. Evil will be judged. Faithfulness will be rewarded. Christ will reign forever.

OUR WITNESS TODAY

What does this vision of the seven trumpets mean for us today? Several truths emerge:

First, our prayers matter more than we realize. When we pray, we participate in God's cosmic purposes. Our prayers for justice, for the gospel's advance, for Christ's return—they're being gathered in heaven's censers, mingling with the incense of Christ's intercession.

Second, God's judgments serve as warnings. The trumpets remind us that God takes sin seriously. Natural disasters, political upheaval, spiritual emptiness—these can all serve as divine megaphones calling people to repentance before the final judgment.

Third, the gospel remains bittersweet. Like John, we find sweetness in receiving and sharing God's Word. But we also experience bitterness when that word is rejected. Both experiences are part of faithful ministry.

Fourth, the church's witness follows Christ's pattern. Like the two witnesses, we testify to the truth, may suffer for that testimony, but ultimately experience vindication. Even when the church appears defeated, God raises it to new life.

Finally, Christ's kingdom will prevail. No matter how dominant evil appears, the kingdoms of this world will become the kingdom of our Lord. History is moving toward the day when Christ will reign visibly over all creation.

QUESTIONS FOR REFLECTION

1. How does seeing the connection between prayer and God's actions change your perspective on prayer?

2. Where do you see God's "megaphone" warnings in our world today? How should believers respond to these signs?

3. In what ways have you experienced the bittersweet nature of God's Word in your own life?

4. Where do you see the church's witness being rejected today, and how does the story of the two witnesses encourage you?

5. How does the certainty of Christ's coming kingdom affect your view of current world events?

PRAYER RESPONSE

Sovereign Lord,

Your judgments are just and true. When we see the brokenness in our world, help us to recognize Your warnings and calls to repentance. Give us courage to proclaim Your truth, even when it brings opposition.

Thank You for gathering our prayers and using them in Your divine purposes. Help us to pray with greater faith and persistence, knowing that our prayers participate in Your work in the world.

As we await the final trumpet, keep us faithful in our witness. When the church seems defeated, remind us that vindication is coming. And when we grow weary, turn our eyes to that glorious day when the kingdoms of this world will become the kingdom of our Lord and of His Christ.

In the name of the coming King, Amen.

VICTORY DECLARATION

We stand confident today knowing that:

- Our prayers are powerful weapons in God's hands.
- God's warnings demonstrate His mercy even in judgment.
- The church's witness, though opposed, will ultimately triumph.
- Christ's kingdom will overcome all earthly kingdoms.
- The God who began the good work of redemption will bring it to completion.

Therefore, we will pray without ceasing, witness without fear, and wait without wavering for the day when Christ will reign forever and ever!

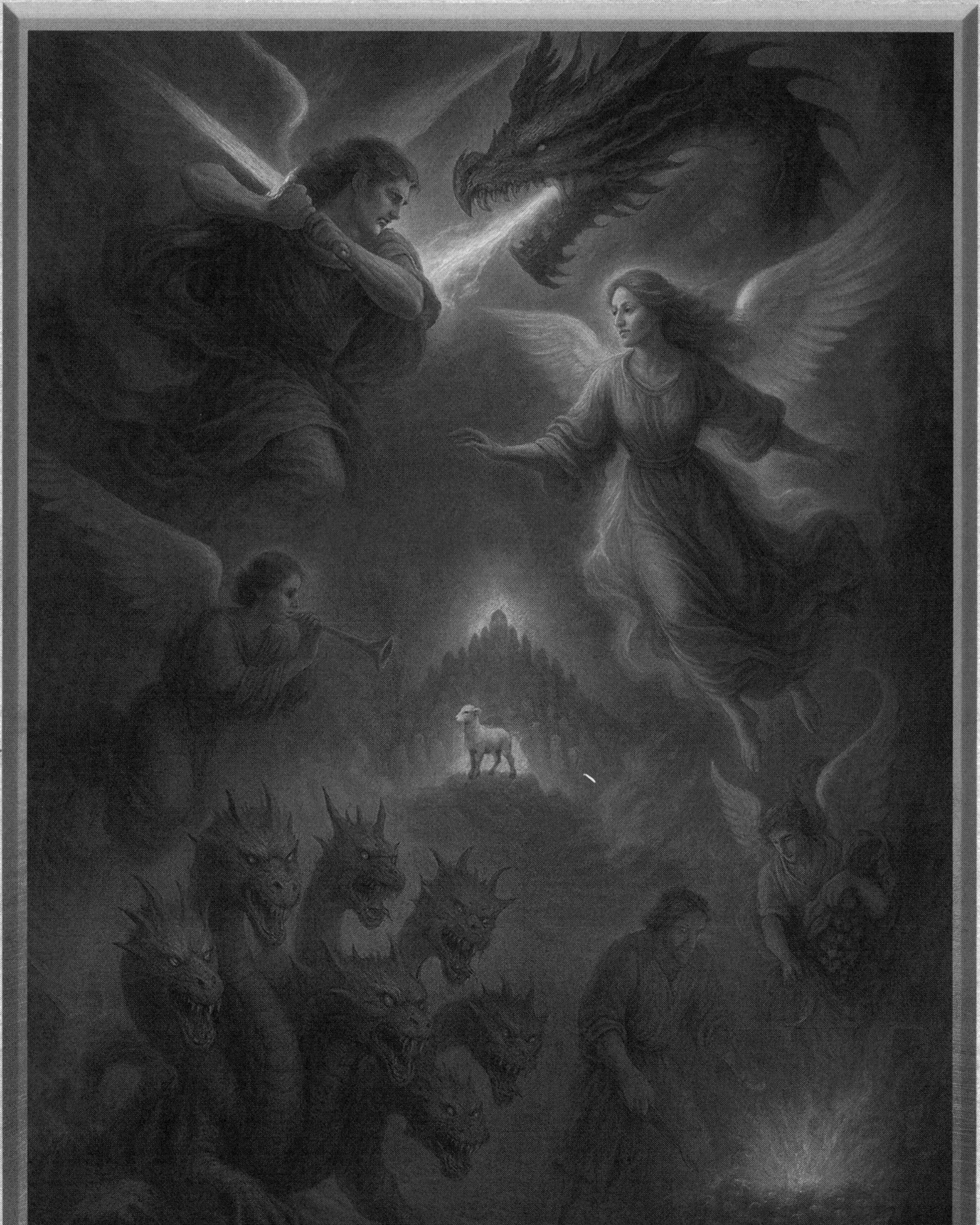

PART FIVE

COSMIC BATTLE (REVELATION 12-14)

Begin by reading Revelation 12:1-14:20

Making It Personal

When you watch the news, the conflicts you see might appear to be primarily political, economic, or cultural. But what if there's a deeper dimension to our world's struggles? What if behind all human conflicts lies an ancient cosmic battle? Revelation 12–14 pulls back the curtain on this spiritual reality, revealing a cosmic war that began before creation and continues to this day. Understanding this unseen battle helps us recognize what's truly at stake in our everyday choices and challenges.

The Woman and the Dragon

"A great sign appeared in heaven..." With these words, Revelation shifts from the trumpet judgments to a series of seven signs. The first of these presents a dramatic scene unlike anything we might expect.

Most of us are familiar with the traditional Christmas story—Mary and Joseph in Bethlehem, no room at the inn, shepherds watching their flocks, angels singing "Glory to God in the highest." But Revelation 12 unveils a cosmic dimension to Christ's birth that rarely makes it into our nativity scenes.

John sees a great sign in heaven: a woman clothed with the sun, with the moon under her feet and a crown of twelve stars. She is pregnant and crying out in birth pains. Then another sign appears: a great red dragon with seven heads and ten horns, and seven crowns on his heads. The dragon stands before the woman, waiting to devour her child the moment it is born.

This is not the Christmas story we tell our children—but it's the Christmas story as heaven sees it. Behind the peaceful scene in Bethlehem was a cosmic battle. The birth of Christ wasn't just a tender moment in human history; it was a decisive moment in the war between God and Satan.

INTERPRETIVE PERSPECTIVES: The Woman

In the ancient world, dragons were widely recognized symbols of chaos and evil. Several elements in Revelation's description of the dragon connect to historical and biblical imagery:

Seven heads and ten horns: This imagery recalls Daniel's vision in Daniel 7, where beasts with multiple heads and horns represented successive world empires. The dragon, then, represents satanic power working through political systems.

Red color: Red symbolizes bloodshed and violence, reflecting Satan's nature as "a murderer from the beginning" (John 8:44).

Stars swept down: This may reference Isaiah 14:12–15, which describes Lucifer's fall: "How you have fallen from heaven, morning star, son of the dawn!"

Ancient serpent: This explicitly identifies the dragon with the Genesis 3 serpent who tempted Eve, establishing continuity in Satan's opposition to God's purposes from Eden to the end times.

These details emphasize that the conflict described is both ancient (extending to creation) and comprehensive (involving the spiritual and political realms).

Who are these three figures in John's vision? The woman likely represents the true Israel, God's covenant people from whom the Messiah came. Her adornment with sun, moon, and stars recalls Joseph's dream in Genesis 37, where these celestial bodies represented Jacob (Israel) and his family—the twelve stars symbolizing the twelve tribes of Israel.

The male child is clearly Jesus Christ. He is destined to "rule all nations with a rod of iron," a clear reference to Messianic prophecies like Psalm 2. After His birth, He is "caught up to God and to His throne," referring to Christ's ascension after His resurrection.

The red dragon is explicitly identified as "that ancient serpent called the devil, or Satan, who leads the whole world astray." His seven heads with seven crowns symbolize his claim to

universal authority, while his ten horns represent his power. His tail sweeps a third of the stars from the sky, possibly referring to the angels who fell with him in his original rebellion.

BEHIND THE SCENES

Satan has opposed God's purposes from the beginning. When God promised that the offspring of the woman would crush the serpent's head (Genesis 3:15), Satan determined to destroy that offspring. Throughout Israel's history, we see repeated attempts to wipe out the Messianic line:

When Pharaoh ordered the death of all Hebrew boys, he was acting as Satan's agent. When Queen Athaliah tried to destroy the royal line of David, it was another satanic attempt to prevent the Messiah's birth. When Haman plotted to exterminate all Jews, Satan was behind it. And when Herod ordered the slaughter of Bethlehem's infant boys, it was the dragon standing ready to devour the child.

But Satan failed. The woman's child was born and, despite Satan's attempts to destroy Him through crucifixion, was raised from the dead and ascended to God's throne. Even Satan's apparent victory at the cross turned into his decisive defeat.

HISTORICAL BACKGROUND: The Dragon

In the ancient world, dragons were widely recognized symbols of chaos and evil. Several elements in Revelation's description of the dragon connect to historical and biblical imagery:

Seven heads and ten horns: This imagery recalls Daniel's vision in Daniel 7, where beasts with multiple heads and horns represented successive world empires. The dragon, then, represents satanic power working through political systems.

Red color: Red symbolizes bloodshed and violence, reflecting Satan's nature as "a murderer from the beginning" (John 8:44).

Stars swept down: This may reference Isaiah 14:12–15, which describes Lucifer's fall: "How you have fallen from heaven, morning star, son of the dawn!"

Ancient serpent: This explicitly identifies the dragon with the Genesis 3 serpent who tempted Eve, establishing continuity in Satan's opposition to God's purposes from Eden to the end times.

These details emphasize that the conflict described is both ancient (extending to creation) and comprehensive (involving the spiritual and political realms).

SATAN'S TACTICS TODAY

John then sees a war break out in heaven. Michael and his angels fight against the dragon and his angels. The dragon is defeated and thrown down to earth, along with his angels. This expulsion triggers rejoicing in heaven but brings woe to the earth, "because the devil has gone down to you in great anger, knowing that his time is short."

When did this expulsion occur? Some place it at Satan's original fall, before human history began. Others link it to Christ's victory at the cross. Either way, the result is the same: Satan now operates in the earthly realm, filled with fury because he knows his time is limited.

John hears a loud voice in heaven declaring the basis of victory: "They triumphed over him by the blood of the Lamb and by the word of their testimony; they did not love their lives so much as to shrink from death." This powerful statement reveals the three weapons that defeat Satan:

The blood of the Lamb—Christ's sacrificial death provides the foundation for all spiritual victory. Satan is the accuser, but Christ's blood silences his accusations. When Satan points to our sin, we point to our Savior.

The word of testimony—Our verbal witness to Christ's saving work extends His victory. Satan hates the gospel because it's the power of God for salvation. Every time we share our testimony, we advance against Satan's kingdom.

Sacrificial commitment—Not loving our lives "so much as to shrink from death" means valuing Christ above everything, even life itself. Satan has no answer for the believer who says, "Kill me if you must; I will not deny my Lord."

Frustrated in his attempts to defeat Christ, the dragon turns his rage against the woman—God's people. He pursues her into the wilderness, but God has prepared a place of refuge for her. Satan spews water like a river from his mouth, trying to sweep her away, but the earth helps the woman by swallowing the water.

WORD STUDY: The Accuser

Revelation 12:10 identifies Satan as "the accuser of our brothers and sisters, who accuses them before our God day and night." The Greek word for "accuser" (katēgoros) is a legal term from which we get our English word "category."

In ancient courts, an accuser would categorize someone under the law they had broken. Satan's role as accuser is dramatically portrayed in Job 1–2, where he appears before God to argue that Job only serves God for selfish reasons.

Satan's accusations typically take three forms:

1. **To God against believers:** "They don't really love you; their faith is insincere."
2. **To believers about God:** "God doesn't really love you; His ways aren't good."
3. **To believers about themselves:** "You've failed too much; you're not worthy to be God's child."

Christ's blood provides the decisive answer to all Satan's accusations: "Who shall bring any charge against God's elect? It is God who justifies. Who is to condemn? Christ Jesus is the one who died—more than that, who was raised" (Romans 8:33–34).

This vivid imagery depicts Satan's ongoing attempts to destroy the church through persecution, false teaching, and cultural pressure. The wilderness represents times of testing and hardship, but also God's provision and protection. The flood from the dragon's mouth likely symbolizes overwhelming opposition—accusations, lies, slander, and cultural hostility.

Yet God preserves His people. The earth swallowing the river may represent how God often uses natural means and human institutions to protect His church. Throughout history, we've seen how persecution often strengthens rather than destroys the faith community.

Enraged by his failure to destroy the woman, the dragon "went off to wage war against the rest of her offspring—those who keep God's commands and hold fast their testimony about Jesus." This is where we find ourselves today—targets in Satan's ongoing war against God's people.

OVERCOMING EVIL

This cosmic perspective transforms how we understand our struggles. The opposition we face as Christians isn't primarily political, cultural, or personal—it's spiritual. Satan opposes us because we belong to Christ. Our struggles are part of a conflict that began before creation and will continue until Christ returns.

This doesn't mean we should see a demon behind every difficulty or blame Satan for all our problems. Much of our suffering comes from living in a fallen world or from our own sinful choices. But we must recognize that beneath the visible conflicts in our world lies an invisible spiritual battle.

How should we live in light of this cosmic war? Several principles emerge:

First, we must maintain proper perspective. Satan is a defeated foe. Christ has already won the decisive victory through His death and resurrection. Satan knows his time is short and his doom is certain. Though he rages against God's people, he cannot ultimately prevail.

Second, we must use our spiritual weapons. The blood of the Lamb, the word of our testimony, and sacrificial commitment—these are the weapons that overcome Satan. We don't fight with worldly weapons but with faith in Christ's finished work, bold witness to His saving power, and wholehearted devotion to His kingdom.

Third, we must expect opposition. If Satan opposed Christ, he will certainly oppose Christ's followers. Peter warns us not to be surprised at the "fiery trial" as though something strange were happening (1 Peter 4:12). Opposition is normal in a cosmic war.

Finally, we must trust God's protection. The woman was given wings to fly to the wilderness "where she would be taken care of." God preserves His people through every assault. Though Satan wages war against us, he can only go as far as God permits. Our lives are in God's hands, not Satan's.

SYSTEMS AGAINST GOD

After failing to destroy the woman (God's people) in chapter 12, the dragon takes a new approach. Standing on the seashore, he summons two powerful allies to help him wage war against the saints. These beasts—one from the sea and one from the earth—represent the primary ways Satan attacks the church: through political power and deceptive ideology.

The word "antichrist" often comes to mind when we read this chapter. While this specific term doesn't appear in Revelation, the concept certainly does. The Bible uses "antichrist" in at least four ways:

First, antichrist can refer to an evil empire or political power that opposes God's people. Second, it can mean the evil spirit of the age that works against Christ's purposes. Third, it represents literal persons throughout history who foreshadow the final antichrist. Fourth, it refers to the final person who will embody satanic power before Christ returns.

As we examine these beasts, we should remember they're not just future realities but present powers at work in our world today.

CROSS REFERENCE: Antichrist in Scripture

Though the term "antichrist" never appears in Revelation, it occurs in John's letters with important meanings:

1 John 2:18: "Dear children, this is the last hour; and as you have heard that the antichrist is coming, even now many antichrists have come."

1 John 2:22: "Who is the liar? It is whoever denies that Jesus is the Christ. Such a person is the antichrist—denying the Father and the Son."

1 John 4:3: "Every spirit that does not acknowledge Jesus is not from God. This is the spirit of the antichrist, which you have heard is coming and even now is already in the world."

2 John 1:7: "I say this because many deceivers, who do not acknowledge Jesus Christ as coming in the flesh, have gone out into the world. Any such person is the deceiver and the antichrist."

These passages reveal that "antichrist" refers to both a future individual and a present reality manifested in false teaching and opposition to Christ. The beasts in Revelation 13 elaborate on this concept without using the specific term.

MARK OF THE BEAST REALITY

The first beast rises from the sea—a symbol of chaos and the masses of humanity. This beast combines features of the four beasts from Daniel 7, which represented successive world empires. It has ten horns and seven heads, mirroring the dragon's appearance, which shows its satanic origin. The beast bears "blasphemous names" and receives its power, throne, and authority from the dragon.

One of the beast's heads appears to have a fatal wound that has healed—perhaps an allusion to Nero, who committed suicide in AD 68 but was rumored to return. More likely, it symbolizes the recurring pattern of empires that fall only to be replaced by new ones. The Assyrian Empire fell, but Babylon rose. Babylon fell, but Persia rose. Persia fell, but Greece rose. Greece fell, but Rome rose. Throughout history, when one beast-like empire falls, another rises to take its place.

The whole world marvels at and worships both the dragon and the beast. The beast speaks "proud words and blasphemies" against God, wages war against the saints, and exercises authority over every tribe, people, language, and nation. All whose names are not written in the Lamb's Book of Life worship the beast.

This beast represents political power that demands ultimate allegiance—the kind of power that puts itself in God's place and persecutes those who refuse to worship it. In John's day, it was Imperial Rome with its emperor cult. In our day, it appears as any political system that demands absolute loyalty and persecutes dissenters.

The second beast rises from the earth. Unlike the first beast, which emerges from chaos, this one comes from settled ground. It has two horns like a lamb but speaks like a dragon—appearing gentle but speaking Satan's lies. This beast serves the first beast, performing great signs and wonders to deceive humanity into worshiping the first beast.

This second beast represents false religion, propaganda, and ideologies that support oppressive political power. In John's day, it was the imperial cult with its priests and propaganda machine. Today, it manifests in ideologies that justify state power and delegitimize Christian faith.

This beast deceives through signs and wonders. Throughout history, false religions have used apparent miracles to validate their claims. But signs alone aren't sufficient evidence of divine approval. Moses warned Israel:

> "If a prophet, or one who foretells by dreams, appears among you and announces to you a sign or wonder, and if the sign or wonder spoken of takes place, and the prophet says, 'Let us follow other gods'… You must not listen to the words of that prophet or dreamer. The LORD your God is testing you to find out whether you love him with all your heart and with all your soul." (Deuteronomy 13:1-3)

The ultimate test isn't whether a religious system produces signs but whether it leads people to the true God revealed in Jesus Christ.

The second beast requires everyone to receive a mark on their right hand or forehead to participate in economic life—without this mark, no one can buy or sell. This mark is "the name of the beast or the number of its name," identified cryptically as 666.

WORD STUDY: The Number 666

Few symbols in Revelation have generated more speculation than the infamous number 666. Several interpretations have been proposed:

Numerical Symbolism: Six falls short of seven (the number of completeness). Three sixes represent "complete incompleteness"—the ultimate human attempt to imitate God that always falls short.

Gematria: In ancient languages, letters had numerical values. In Hebrew gematria, the letters in "Nero Caesar" add up to 666, suggesting the beast embodies Nero-like oppression.

Human Number: Revelation calls it "the number of man," possibly indicating that despite its claims to divinity, the beast is merely human and finite.

Symbolic Warning: Rather than identifying a specific individual, the number warns against any system that claims ultimate allegiance.

In the idealist interpretation, 666 represents the perpetual human tendency to elevate human systems to divine status—a temptation present in every generation.

What is this mark? Throughout church history, people have identified it with various systems: numerology based on people's names, barcodes, microchips, vaccines, and more. But understanding the mark requires looking at its Old Testament background.

In Deuteronomy 6, God instructed Israel: "These commandments ... are to be on your hearts ... Tie them as symbols on your hands and bind them on your foreheads." This wasn't a literal mark but a symbol of complete devotion—their thoughts (forehead) and actions (hands) were to be shaped by God's Word.

Similarly, the mark of the beast isn't necessarily a visible, physical mark but a symbol of allegiance to the beast's system. It represents conforming one's thoughts and actions to the

demands of godless political power. The economic aspect—not being able to buy or sell without the mark—reflects how totalitarian systems exclude dissenters from economic participation.

In John's day, participation in the imperial cult was often necessary for economic activity. Trade guilds required members to honor the patron deity and the emperor. Christians who refused faced economic hardship. Throughout history, believers have faced similar pressure to compromise their faith for economic survival.

Satan cannot create; he can only counterfeit. In Revelation 13, we see his attempt to mimic the Trinity:

> The dragon (Satan) counterfeits God the Father. The beast from the sea counterfeits God the Son, even experiencing a "resurrection" from a fatal wound. The beast from the earth counterfeits God the Holy Spirit, directing worship to the first beast just as the Spirit glorifies Christ.

This unholy trinity demands the worship that belongs only to the true God. Satan has always wanted what belongs to God. Isaiah 14 depicts his fall as rooted in the desire to "make myself like the Most High." His temptation to Adam and Eve was "you will be like God." His ultimate aim is to receive the worship due to God alone.

FAITHFUL RESISTANCE

Chapter 14 presents a dramatic contrast to the beasts and their followers. John sees the Lamb standing on Mount Zion with the 144,000 who have the Father's name written on their foreheads. Instead of the mark of the beast, they bear the name of God.

These 144,000 sing a new song that only they can learn. They are described as those "who did not defile themselves with women, for they remained virgins." This is symbolic language for spiritual purity—those who have not committed spiritual adultery by worshiping the beast. They follow the Lamb wherever he goes and have been purchased from among mankind as firstfruits to God and the Lamb.

After this vision of the redeemed, John sees three angels with messages for the earth's inhabitants:

The first angel proclaims the eternal gospel to every nation, tribe, language, and people—calling them to fear God, give Him glory, and worship Him as Creator. This reminds us that even in the darkest times, the gospel continues to go forth.

The second angel announces, "Fallen! Fallen is Babylon the Great!" Babylon represents the world system with its seductive materialism and anti-God values. Though it appears powerful and permanent, its ultimate collapse is certain.

The third angel warns about the consequences of worshiping the beast and receiving his mark. Those who do so "will drink the wine of God's fury" and "will be tormented with burning sulfur." This stark warning emphasizes the eternal consequences of our spiritual allegiances.

These angelic proclamations are followed by a voice from heaven declaring, "Blessed are the dead who die in the Lord from now on." While the world may see martyrdom as defeat, heaven sees it as victory. Those who remain faithful to death receive rest from their labor.

The chapter concludes with two harvest images: the harvest of grain (representing the gathering of believers) and the harvest of grapes (depicting God's judgment on unbelievers). These images remind us that history is moving toward a definite conclusion where both salvation and judgment will be complete.

LIVING COUNTER-CULTURALLY

What does this vision of the dragon and beasts mean for us today? Several truths emerge:

First, we must recognize the beasts in our midst. Political absolutism and deceptive ideology aren't just future threats—they're present realities. Whenever a political system demands ultimate allegiance, it becomes beast-like. Whenever ideology justifies oppression and excludes dissenters, the second beast is at work.

Second, we must develop endurance. Verse 10 ends with the call: "This calls for patient endurance and faithfulness on the part of God's people." Endurance means the ability to withstand hardship without giving up. As pressure grows to conform to anti-Christian systems, believers need spiritual stamina.

Third, we must cultivate wisdom. After describing the second beast and the mark, John writes, "This calls for wisdom." Wisdom means discernment—the ability to distinguish truth from error, genuine faith from counterfeits. In a world of deception, believers need wisdom to navigate competing claims.

Fourth, we must maintain undivided allegiance to Christ. The mark of the beast represents complete allegiance to a godless system. As believers, we bear a different mark—the seal of God's Spirit that identifies us as His (Ephesians 1:13–14). Our thoughts and actions must demonstrate our allegiance to Christ alone.

Finally, we must remember that Satan and his beasts are already defeated. Despite their temporary power, their ultimate downfall is certain. The Lamb who was slain will triumph over every beast-like system that opposes Him.

STANDING IN VICTORY

Our cosmic battle isn't fought on a level playing field. We don't face the dragon and beasts in our own strength, wondering who might prevail. We enter the conflict knowing the outcome is already decided—Christ has won the decisive victory through His death and resurrection.

This perspective transforms how we approach spiritual warfare. We don't fight for victory but from victory. Satan's most potent weapons—accusation, deception, and intimidation—have all been disarmed by Christ's finished work. When Satan accuses, we point to the blood of the Lamb. When Satan deceives, we cling to the truth of God's Word. When Satan intimidates, we remember that "greater is He that is in you than he that is in the world" (1 John 4:4).

Standing in victory means living with confidence rather than fear. We recognize Satan's limitations—he can roar like a lion, but he cannot devour those who resist him, standing firm in the faith (1 Peter 5:8–9). He may win battles, but he has lost the war.

Standing in victory also means living with expectation rather than resignation. We know that one day, the God of peace will crush Satan under our feet (Romans 16:20). This promise isn't just about a future triumph but about God's ongoing work through His church to push back the darkness and establish His kingdom.

Therefore, we proclaim the gospel boldly, worship purely, love sacrificially, and endure faithfully—knowing that our labor in the Lord is not in vain. In the cosmic battle that rages around us, we are more than conquerors through Him who loved us (Romans 8:37).

QUESTIONS FOR REFLECTION

1. How does seeing your struggles as part of a cosmic war change your perspective on the challenges you face?

2. In what ways have you experienced Satan's accusations, and how can you more effectively apply "the blood of the Lamb" to silence those accusations?

3. What specific steps can you take to strengthen your testimony about Jesus in the face of opposition?

4. Where do you see the influence of the first beast (oppressive political power) in today's world?

5. How have you encountered the second beast (deceptive ideology) in your own cultural context?

6. In what specific areas of life do you face pressure to "take the mark"—to conform your thoughts and actions to godless systems?

PRAYER RESPONSE

Sovereign Lord,

Thank You for revealing the true nature of the conflict we face. Help us to see beyond the visible struggles to the invisible war that rages around us. Remind us that our battle is not against flesh and blood but against the spiritual forces of evil.

Thank You that Satan is a defeated foe. Though he rages against Your people, his time is short and his doom is certain. Help us to stand firm against his schemes, clothed in the full armor You provide.

When accusations come, remind us of the blood of the Lamb that silences every charge against us. When opposition arises, give us courage to maintain our testimony about Jesus. When persecution threatens, strengthen our commitment to follow You whatever the cost.

We rejoice that the victory is already won. Satan has been thrown down, and soon he will be thrown out forever. Until that day, preserve us by Your mighty hand.

In the name of Christ our Champion, Amen.

VICTORY DECLARATION

We stand confident today knowing that:

- Christ has defeated Satan through His death and resurrection.
- The blood of the Lamb silences every accusation against us.
- Our testimony extends Christ's victory in the world.
- God preserves His people through every assault.
- Satan's time is short and his doom is certain.

Therefore, we will stand firm in faith, bold in witness, and unwavering in our commitment to Christ, knowing that the One who is in us is greater than the one who is in the world!

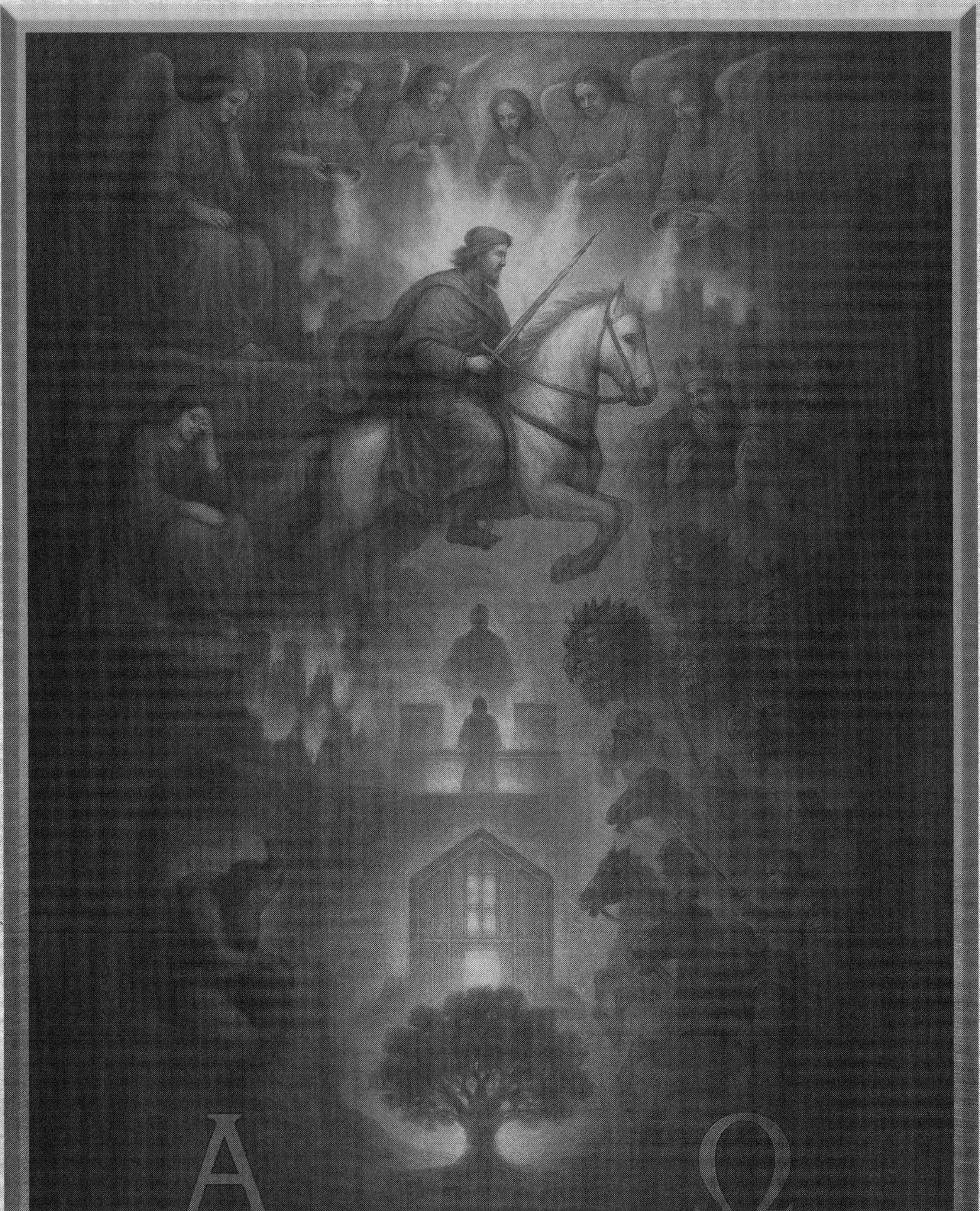
A
Ω

PART SIX

FINAL VICTORY (REVELATION 15-22)

Begin by reading Revelation 15:1-22:21

Making It Personal

Have you ever watched a movie where evil seems to have triumphed, only to discover in the final scenes that the hero had a plan all along? As the closing sequences unfold, everything changes—justice prevails, evil is defeated, and hope is restored. The final chapters of Revelation tell the ultimate version of this story. After the cosmic conflict with all its hardship and opposition, God's victory is revealed in all its glory. These chapters assure us that no matter how dire circumstances may appear, God's purpose prevails, Christ's reign is established, and all things are made new.

Seven Bowls Understanding

The judgment of the seven bowls brings the seven plagues, which are described as "the last." Those who interpret Revelation chronologically understand "last" to mean these judgments follow the seven seals and seven trumpets in sequence. However, from an idealist perspective, since these three sets of judgments cover the same events from different angles, the seven bowls are the "last" of the three visions about divine judgment given to John—not necessarily last in historical chronology.

INTERPRETIVE PERSPECTIVES: The Three Sets of Judgment

The relationship between the seals, trumpets, and bowls can be understood in different ways:

Sequential View: Each set follows chronologically after the previous one—seals first, then trumpets, finally bowls. This creates a linear progression of increasingly severe judgments.

Parallel View: Each set covers the same events from different perspectives, with each new cycle adding detail and intensity:

- **Seals (one-fourth affected):** Basic overview of patterns throughout history
- **Trumpets (one-third affected):** More intense view with increased warning
- elements
- **Bowls (complete):** Final, most intense perspective with no more partial judgments

Telescopic View: The seventh seal opens into the seven trumpets, and the seventh trumpet opens into the seven bowls—creating a nested structure where each set emerges from the previous.

The idealist approach favors the parallel view, understanding these judgments as different angles on the same realities throughout history, with the bowls representing the final, complete execution of God's judgment.

Before the bowls are poured out, John sees something like a sea of glass mingled with fire. Remember, the sea symbolizes chaos, so a sea of glass shows that God is going to calm the chaos. And the sea of glass is mingled with fire, which represents God's purifying judgment. How is God going to calm the chaos? By bringing judgment on the wicked.

Standing by this sea of glass are God's people—those who conquered the beast with its image and number. They have harps in their hands and are singing a song of victory. Just as Moses, the servant of God, delivered God's people from bondage in Egypt, so shall Jesus, the Lamb of God, deliver God's people from sin, Satan, and the beasts!

"Great and amazing are your deeds, O Lord God the Almighty! Just and true are your ways, O King of the nations!" These saints don't sing in protest of God's judgments but in affirmation of them. This is significant because some people say they cannot worship a God who judges and sends people to hell. Yet here, God's people in heaven have no problem worshiping God as He judges, because they know His ways are just and true.

WORD STUDY: Song of Moses

The "song of Moses and the song of the Lamb" connects two of history's greatest deliverances:

The original Song of Moses (Exodus 15:1–18, ESV) was sung after God delivered Israel through the Red Sea, destroying Pharaoh's army. It celebrated God's power over Egypt: "I will sing to the LORD, for he has triumphed gloriously; the horse and his rider he has thrown into the sea."

By combining this with "the song of the Lamb," Revelation shows that Christ's redemption fulfills and surpasses the exodus deliverance. The exodus was a physical deliverance of one nation from political bondage; Christ's work is a spiritual deliverance of people from every nation from the bondage of sin.

This combined song emphasizes several attributes of God:

- His amazing deeds (omnipotence)
- His just and true ways (righteousness)
- His holiness (moral perfection)
- His worthiness of universal worship (sovereignty)

The exodus was a defining event for Israel; Christ's redemption is the defining event for all humanity.

Next, the bowls of wrath are poured. In chapter 16, John sees the seven angels coming from the sanctuary dressed like Christ as His representatives. When the angels receive the seven bowls full of God's wrath, the sanctuary is filled with the smoke of God's glory. God's wrath is so holy and just that His glory fills the heavenly sanctuary much like God's glory filled the earthly sanctuary in Exodus after it was built. Moses could not even enter the earthly tabernacle, and the angels could not enter this heavenly tabernacle until the plagues were finished.

The angels pour out the bowls. The seals affected a quarter of the people, while the trumpets affected a third. Those were partial judgments to give people an opportunity to repent. But these bowl judgments are for those who refuse to repent!

The first five bowls echo the plagues in Egypt (similar to the seven trumpets). There are sores on those who bear the mark of the beast. The sea and the rivers become like blood. The sun scorched the people with fire and fierce heat, yet people still do not repent. Darkness comes upon the land. People gnawed their tongues and cursed God for their pain and sores. Can you imagine gnawing your tongue while trying to curse God? They would rather curse God than repent.

This is happening now. Despite all the disasters, war, pain, and suffering, people still refuse to turn to God. One of the purposes of pain and suffering is to awaken our need for God. It should cause us to run to Him, not run from Him.

The sixth bowl dries up the river Euphrates so that the kings can gather from the east for war. This gathering of kings points to the gathering of the armies from the dragon and the beasts against the Lamb in the final battle of Armageddon.

HISTORICAL BACKGROUND: Armageddon

The term "Armageddon" appears only once in Scripture (Revelation 16:16) and has captured the imagination of many. Understanding its background helps clarify its meaning:

Geographic Significance: The name derives from "Har Megiddo" (Mountain of Megiddo). Megiddo was an ancient city overlooking the plain of Jezreel (Esdraelon), a strategic location that witnessed numerous battles throughout Israel's history.

Historical Battles: Megiddo and its surrounding plain saw many significant conflicts:

- Deborah and Barak defeated Sisera's army there (Judges 5)
- Gideon confronted the Midianites nearby (Judges 7)
- King Josiah was killed in battle against Pharaoh Necho at Megiddo (2 Kings 23:29–30)

Symbolic Meaning: Interestingly, there is no actual mountain at Megiddo—only a tell (archaeological mound) and a plain. This suggests that "Har Megiddo" carries symbolic significance beyond geography.

In the idealist interpretation, Armageddon represents the final confrontation between good and evil, the decisive spiritual battle where God's sovereignty is ultimately displayed—not necessarily a literal geographic location for an end-time war.

Armageddon means "the mountain of Megiddo." Megiddo is a two-day walk from Jerusalem and was the battleground where God delivered Israel from her enemies during the days of Judges. But there's no mountain in Megiddo—it's a plain. So why does Armageddon mean "the mountain of Megiddo"? Mountains symbolize strength. Israel saw God as their mountain that they could run to for deliverance.

Therefore, Armageddon represents the place where God will deliver His people from a superior enemy. God is our mountain of deliverance! God is our Armageddon! Armageddon won't be a battle but a slaughter. Robert Mounce writes, "Wherever it takes place, Armageddon is symbolic of the final overthrow of all the forces of evil by the might and power of God."

The seventh bowl brings the terrible Day of the Lord with lightning, thunder, earthquake, and hailstones weighing one hundred pounds each. This sounds so severe, but verse 6 (chapter 16) says that it is what they deserve. Verse 7 says that God's judgments are true and just! You will either get mercy or justice. Nobody gets injustice.

Sin deserves justice. Since God is holy, He must judge sin. Sin against an eternal God deserves eternal judgment. Even if it appears that the wicked are getting away with their evil or it seems that you are not reaping what you have sown, there is a Day coming when all accounts will be settled. No one gets away scot-free! Judgment is coming!

BABYLON'S FALL

Following the seventh bowl judgment, John is shown "the judgment of the great prostitute who is seated on many waters." This prostitute, identified as "Babylon the Great," represents any evil and idolatrous system that opposes God's kingdom.

John sees her sitting on a scarlet beast full of blasphemous names, adorned with expensive clothing and jewelry, holding a golden cup full of abominations, and drunk with the blood of the saints. This imagery conveys her wealth, corruption, and role in persecuting believers.

CROSS REFERENCE: Babylon in Scripture

Babylon appears throughout Scripture as a symbol of organized opposition to God:

Genesis 11:1–9: Babel (Babylon) was where humanity first organized to rebel against God through the tower

Isaiah 13–14, Jeremiah 50–51: Prophetic judgments against historical Babylon emphasize God's opposition to its pride and brutality

1 Peter 5:13: The early church used "Babylon" as a code name for Rome, the oppressive empire of their day

Revelation 17-18: Babylon represents all human systems opposed to God—political, economic, and religious

These references show that "Babylon" is more than a single historical entity; it represents humanity's recurrent attempt to organize society apart from God. Each historical manifestation (ancient Babylon, Rome, and subsequent empires) displays similar characteristics: pride, wealth, idolatry, and persecution of God's people.

In John's day, Babylon clearly represented Rome, the dominant empire that persecuted the church and demanded allegiance that belonged only to God. But Babylon transcends any single historical entity. It represents the world system in every generation—the organized patterns of life and thought that oppose God's rule.

The prostitute's name is written on her forehead: "Babylon the great, mother of prostitutes and of earth's abominations." Just as God's people receive a seal on their foreheads showing their allegiance to God, the followers of Babylon bear her mark. The contrast couldn't be clearer: we serve either God or Babylon, Christ or the world.

Babylon seduces people to commit sexual immorality and become drunk with wickedness. This isn't merely about literal sexual sin, though that's included. The primary reference is to spiritual adultery—being unfaithful to God by giving our ultimate allegiance to created things.

In Revelation 18, an angel announces Babylon's fall: "Fallen, fallen is Babylon the great!" The repetition emphasizes the certainty of her judgment. Though Babylon appears mighty and permanent, her collapse is inevitable. The imagery recalls Old Testament prophecies about ancient Babylon's judgment, underscoring that all human kingdoms that oppose God will eventually meet the same fate.

God's people are commanded to "come out of her, my people, lest you take part in her sins, lest you share in her plagues." This doesn't mean physical withdrawal from society but refusing to adopt Babylon's values and practices. We're called to be in the world but not of it—maintaining distinct identities as citizens of God's kingdom while engaging with our culture.

When Babylon falls, three groups respond differently:

The kings of the earth, who committed immorality with her, weep and mourn. The merchants, who grew rich from her, stand far off in fear, lamenting the loss of their market. The shipmasters and sailors, who transported her goods, cry out as their livelihood vanishes.

These responses reveal Babylon's true nature: She creates co-dependent relationships based on power, profit, and prosperity rather than truth and love. When she falls, those who relied on her are devastated because they've built their lives on a false foundation.

But heaven has a different response: "Rejoice over her, O heaven, and you saints and apostles and prophets, for God has given judgment for you against her!" (18:20). Heaven rejoices not out of vindictiveness but because God's justice vindicates His people and establishes His kingdom.

MARRIAGE SUPPER JOY

As Babylon falls, attention shifts to what follows: the marriage supper of the Lamb. Chapter 19 opens with a scene of heavenly celebration. A great multitude cries out, "Hallelujah! Salvation and glory and power belong to our God, for his judgments are true and just; for he has judged the great prostitute who corrupted the earth with her immorality, and has avenged on her the blood of his servants."

The multitude continues, "Hallelujah! For the Lord our God the Almighty reigns. Let us rejoice and exult and give him the glory, for the marriage of the Lamb has come, and his Bride has made herself ready; it was granted her to clothe herself with fine linen, bright and pure"—for the fine linen is the righteous deeds of the saints."

WORD STUDY: Marriage Supper

The "marriage supper of the Lamb" draws on rich biblical imagery: In ancient Jewish weddings, there were typically three phases:

1. **Betrothal** (legal commitment, similar to engagement but legally binding)
2. **Procession** (the groom coming to take his bride to their new home)
3. **Feast** (celebration with family and friends, often lasting days)

Spiritually, these phases correspond to:

1. **Betrothal:** The church is currently betrothed to Christ (2 Corinthians 11:2)
2. **Procession:** Christ will return to take His bride home (John 14:3)
3. **Feast:** The ultimate celebration of union with Christ

The "fine linen, bright and pure" worn by the bride represents "the righteous acts of the saints" (19:8)—not works that earn salvation, but works that flow from salvation as evidence of faith.

This marriage imagery emphasizes Christ's faithful love, the intimacy of believers' relationship with Him, and the joy of eternal communion with Him.

This transition from Babylon's funeral to the Lamb's wedding is significant. Throughout history, two cities compete for humanity's allegiance: Babylon and Jerusalem, the prostitute and the bride. The fall of one coincides with the triumph of the other.

The image of a wedding celebrates the intimate, covenant relationship between Christ and His Church. Marriage in Scripture consistently serves as a metaphor for the relationship between God and His people. Just as marriage unites two into one, salvation unites us with Christ in the closest possible bond.

The angel tells John, "Blessed are those who are invited to the marriage supper of the Lamb." This blessing echoes the first beatitude of Revelation (1:3) and reminds us that participation in this celebration is both a privilege and a joy. Not everyone will attend this wedding; only those

whose names are written in the Lamb's Book of Life—those who have responded to the gospel invitation—will be present.

It's worth noting that the bride "makes herself ready" and is "granted" to wear fine linen, which represents "the righteous deeds of the saints." This balance between divine grace and human responsibility is crucial. We don't earn our place at the marriage supper through good works, but saving faith inevitably produces good works as evidence.

The joy of the marriage supper offers a stark contrast to the destiny of those who align with Babylon. While believers celebrate this intimate union with Christ, unbelievers face "the great supper of God" (19:17-18)—a gruesome image of judgment where birds feast on the flesh of God's enemies. The same event that brings ultimate joy to some brings ultimate judgment to others.

READY FOR HIS RETURN

With the stage set by both Babylon's fall and the announcement of the marriage supper, the focus shifts to Christ's return. John sees heaven opened and a white horse appearing, with its rider called "Faithful and True." In chapter 1, Jesus identified Himself as "the faithful witness"; now He appears as the faithful warrior who executes judgment in righteousness.

The details of Christ's appearance are striking:

His eyes are like flames of fire, penetrating all deception. He wears many crowns, signifying His universal sovereignty. He has a name written that no one knows but Himself, highlighting the mystery of His person that exceeds human comprehension. He is clothed in a robe dipped in blood, not His own blood shed on the cross, but the blood of His enemies in judgment. From His mouth comes a sharp sword with which to strike down the nations, showing that His word alone is sufficient to defeat all opposition.

The armies of heaven follow Him on white horses, clothed in fine linen, white and pure. These armies likely include both angels and saints, united in Christ's triumphant return. On His robe and thigh, He has a name written: "King of kings and Lord of lords"—the ultimate declaration of His supremacy over all human authorities.

This vision of Christ's return stands in stark contrast to His first coming. When Jesus came to Bethlehem, He came in humility as a helpless infant. When He returns, He will come in glory as the conquering King. His first coming was to seek and save the lost; His second coming will be to judge and reign.

The battle against the Beast and the kings of the earth is described with remarkable brevity. There is no extended conflict, no dramatic back-and-forth struggle. The outcome is never in doubt. The Beast and the false prophet are captured and thrown alive into the lake of fire. Their armies are killed by the sword from Christ's mouth. The decisive victory belongs to the Lamb.

Following this victory, an angel seizes Satan, binds him for a thousand years, and throws him into the pit. The purpose is clear: "so that he might not deceive the nations any longer." After the thousand years, he must be released for a little while.

CHRIST'S GLORIOUS APPEARING

When Jesus first came, He came as a baby. He walked the earth as a gentle and peaceful Savior. But Jesus will return as the King who makes war!

As we near the end of the revelation of Jesus Christ, John sees seven visions ("then I saw", depending on your English translation). Seven symbolizes completion. John sees heaven open, and before him is a white horse. This is the first vision. Jesus Christ will be the conquering King. This is what the white horse symbolizes. In ancient times, when a Roman general entered a city as the conqueror, he rode a white stallion to celebrate his triumph. Jesus rode into Jerusalem on a donkey, demonstrating His humility, but the day will come when Jesus will return to this earth riding a white horse as the conqueror!

Jesus is the faithful and true King. Faithful means that He can be trusted and relied upon. He said that He will conquer, judge, and condemn all the ungodly and evil of this world, and He will be faithful to do it. True means the absolute truth as opposed to the lies and deceptions in our world today. The conquest and judgment of Jesus will be true.

Jesus will judge and make war upon the earth in righteousness. His righteousness will be the criteria, the law by which all shall be judged. Your comparison is not with other people. Your comparison is with Jesus! He's the standard. Any person who does not measure up to the righteousness of Jesus Christ will be conquered, judged, and condemned exactly where he or she comes up short. Our only hope is to place our faith in Jesus!

Jesus is the consuming King. His eyes will be like fire symbolizing piercing, penetrating power. He sees everywhere, even in the dark places and behind closed doors. His eyes search the innermost recesses of the heart. Many people use the phrase "the Lord knows my heart" as an excuse. But He does know your heart! He knows all. He is omniscient, and He is able to conquer all those who reject Him and do evil.

Jesus will be wearing many crowns, that is, the royal crowns of rule and authority over many kingdoms. He is coming to conquer all the kingdoms of the earth. He will have a name written somewhere that only He knows. But one name that we know He has is the Word of God. And with that name, He will slaughter His enemies. His robe will be sprinkled with blood. This is not His blood. He already shed His own redemptive blood on the cross. No, this is the blood of His enemies.

CROSS REFERENCE: The Warrior Messiah

While many focus exclusively on Christ's role as the suffering servant in His first coming, the Old Testament also prophesied His return as conquering king:

Psalm 2:9 (ESV): "You shall break them with a rod of iron and dash them in pieces like a potter's vessel."

Isaiah 63:1–6 (ESV): "Who is this who comes from Edom, in crimsoned garments from Bozrah…? It is I, speaking in righteousness, mighty to save… I have trodden the winepress alone… I trampled them in my anger and trod them down in my wrath; their lifeblood spattered on my garments."

Revelation 19:15–16 (ESV): "From his mouth comes a sharp sword with which to strike down the nations, and he will rule them with a rod of iron. He will tread the winepress of the fury of the wrath of God the Almighty. On his robe and on his thigh he has a name written, King of kings and Lord of lords."

Like grapes thrown into a winepress, so will the wicked be thrown into the great winepress of the wrath of God.

A winepress is where grapes are stomped on by foot, and a duct leading to a basin collects the juice. The splattering of juice is a picture of the splattered blood of the wicked who will be destroyed.

These passages remind us that Christ's work of redemption includes both gracious salvation for those who believe and righteous judgment for those who rebel. The meek Lamb who was slain is also the mighty Lion who conquers.

MILLENNIUM PERSPECTIVES

The binding of Satan and the thousand-year reign of Christ described in Revelation 20 have generated significant debate among interpreters. Three major views have emerged regarding this "millennium":

Premillennialism teaches that Christ will return before (pre-) the millennium. According to this view, Christ's second coming initiates a literal thousand-year reign on earth, followed by the final judgment.

Postmillennialism holds that Christ will return after (post-) the millennium. This view suggests that the church's increasing influence will usher in a golden age of Christian dominance, after which Christ will return.

Amillennialism interprets the millennium symbolically. This view understands the "thousand years" as representing the entire church age—the period between Christ's first and second comings.

TEACHING BOX: The Three Millennial Views

Premillennialism

- Christ returns before the millennium begins
- Often includes belief in a pre-tribulation rapture
- Satan bound at Christ's second coming
- Millennium is a literal 1,000-year period on earth
- Followed by Satan's brief release and final judgment
- Strengths: Takes 1,000 years literally; emphasizes Christ's earthly reign
- Key Verses: Revelation 20:1–6; Isaiah 11:6–9; Zechariah 14:9

Postmillennialism

- Christ returns after the millennium ends
- Church's mission increasingly successful
- Gospel gradually transforms culture and nations
- Millennium is a future golden age (not necessarily 1,000 literal years)
- Strengths: Optimistic view of gospel's transformative power
- Key Verses: Psalm 72:8–11; Isaiah 2:2–4; Matthew 13:31–33

Amillennialism

- Millennium is symbolic of the current church age
- Satan bound at Christ's first coming (limiting his ability to deceive)
- Saints reign with Christ now in heaven and spiritually on earth
- Christ returns after this period for final judgment
- Strengths: Simplifies timeline; consistent with "already/not yet" tension
- Key Verses: Matthew 12:29; John 12:31–32; Colossians 2:15

Each view has biblical support and faithful adherents. While important, millennial views should not divide believers who share faith in Christ's return, reign, and ultimate victory.

In this book, we're primarily following an idealist interpretation, which aligns closely with the amillennial view. From this perspective, the millennium is the reign of Christ from heaven in the hearts of believers and His church. This is another way of referring to the current church age.

With this view, Satan is already bound. When was Satan bound? He was bound at the first coming of Jesus. When you read the OT, have you ever wondered why the scope of God's kingdom never expanded beyond Israel? Because Satan was deceiving the nations! But when Jesus came to the earth, He bound Satan so that He and the apostles could cast out demons.

Mark 3:26–27 (ESV): "And if Satan has risen up against himself and is divided, he cannot stand, but is coming to an end. But no one can enter a strong man's house and plunder his goods, unless he first binds the strong man. Then indeed he may plunder his house."

Jesus tied up the strongman, Satan, so that He could plunder believers from his power. The binding of Satan does not mean he is not going around devouring people. What is bound is Satan's capacity to deceive nations, not individuals. The binding of Satan means that he cannot stop the spread of the gospel. After the cross, the gospel of Jesus has spread across the globe, with millions of people from every tribe, language, and nation being added to the kingdom of God.

According to this view, the "first resurrection" refers to the spiritual life believers receive in Christ (John 5:24–25), while the "second resurrection" refers to the bodily resurrection of all people at the end of the age. Those who participate in the first resurrection (salvation) will not be harmed by the "second death" (eternal judgment).

After the thousand years (the church age), Satan will be released briefly. This corresponds to a final rebellion against God's people before Christ returns. This temporary release doesn't indicate that Satan regains the ground he lost at the cross but represents a final, desperate assault against the truth.

Following this final rebellion, Satan is thrown into the lake of fire, where he will be tormented day and night forever. This marks the definitive end of his influence and the beginning of God's unchallenged reign.

FINAL JUDGMENT TRUTH

After Satan's defeat, John sees a great white throne and Him who sits on it. From His presence, earth and sky flee, finding no place. This powerful image communicates that nothing can hide from God's judgment.

The dead, great and small, stand before the throne as books are opened. These books contain the record of every human action, thought, and motive. Another book is opened: the Book of Life, which contains the names of those who belong to Christ through faith.

The dead are judged "according to what they had done as recorded in the books." This does not imply salvation through works; rather, works serve as evidence of faith. As Jesus taught, "By their fruit you will recognize them" (Matthew 7:16). Good works do not save us, but they do reveal the presence of saving faith. John Calvin stated, "Faith alone justifies, but the faith that justifies is never alone."

For those whose names are not written in the Book of Life, the judgment is severe: They are thrown into the lake of fire, which is the second death. This "second death" doesn't mean extinction but eternal separation from God's blessing and presence.

Significantly, even death and Hades are thrown into the lake of fire. This indicates the complete end of death's power and the establishment of a new order where death no longer exists. Paul captures this triumph in 1 Corinthians 15:26: "The last enemy to be destroyed is death."

The reality of final judgment raises important questions: Is it just for God to punish people eternally? Why doesn't He simply annihilate those who reject Him? How can we reconcile God's love with eternal judgment?

While these questions deserve thoughtful engagement, several principles emerge from Scripture:

1. God's justice demands that sin be punished. Because God is infinitely holy, sin against Him carries infinite consequences.
2. Humans are created with eternal souls. We are designed to exist forever, either in God's loving presence or apart from it.
3. God has provided a way of escape through Christ. No one who faces judgment must do so; salvation is freely offered to all who believe.
4. Those in hell continue to reject God. C.S. Lewis insightfully noted that the doors of hell are "locked from the inside"—those who reject God in life would not choose Him in eternity.

The doctrine of final judgment is sobering, but it underscores the seriousness of our choices and the urgency of the gospel. It also affirms that God will ultimately establish perfect justice in a world where justice often seems absent.

All Things New

After the final judgment, John sees "a new heaven and a new earth, for the first heaven and the first earth had passed away, and the sea was no more." This vision fulfills Isaiah's prophecy: "Behold, I will create new heavens and a new earth. The former things will not be remembered, nor will they come to mind" (Isaiah 65:17 NIV).

The absence of the sea signifies the removal of chaos and disorder. In ancient Jewish thought, the sea represented danger and unpredictability. Its absence in the new creation indicates perfect peace and security.

Then John sees "the Holy City, the new Jerusalem, coming down out of heaven from God, prepared as a bride beautifully dressed for her husband." This descent of the city symbolizes the uniting of heaven and earth. The separation between God's dwelling and humanity's dwelling is eliminated as God comes to dwell with His people.

WORD STUDY: New

The Greek word for "new" in "new heaven and new earth" is *kainos*, which emphasizes newness in quality and character rather than simply newness in time (for which *neos* would be used).

This distinction matters because it clarifies that God isn't simply creating another cosmos from scratch; He's transforming and renewing the existing creation. Romans 8:19-22 describes creation "groaning" in anticipation of being "liberated from its bondage to decay," suggesting renovation rather than replacement.

This renewal fulfills God's original purpose. Creation wasn't a failed experiment that God abandons for something better; it's His good work that He redeems and perfects. The new creation represents continuity and discontinuity—the same world made new without sin, suffering, and death.

As theologian N.T. Wright explains, "What God does in Jesus Christ and the Spirit is not to abandon the original creation and make something else instead but rather to bring the original creation through death and out into new life."

A loud voice from the throne announces, "Look! God's dwelling place is now among the people, and he will dwell with them. They will be his people, and God himself will be with them and be their God." This fulfills the covenant formula found throughout Scripture: "I will be their God, and they will be my people" (Leviticus 26:12; Jeremiah 31:33; Ezekiel 37:27).

The voice continues with a profound promise: "He will wipe every tear from their eyes. There will be no more death or mourning or crying or pain, for the old order of things has passed away." This promise addresses the deepest human longing—to be free from suffering and death. It assures us that all the consequences of sin and the fall will be undone in God's new creation.

Then the One seated on the throne declares, "I am making everything new!" This is not a future promise but a present reality. God is already at work renewing all things through Christ. As Paul writes, "If anyone is in Christ, the new creation has come: The old has gone, the new is here!" (2 Corinthians 5:17, NIV).

The vision continues with a detailed description of the New Jerusalem in 21:9–27. The city is described as having:

- Walls great and high with twelve gates named after the twelve tribes of Israel
- Foundations adorned with precious stones and named after the twelve apostles
- Dimensions that form a perfect cube—12,000 stadia in length, width, and height
- Construction of pure gold, clear as glass
- Streets of pure gold, as transparent as glass

This elaborate description employs rich symbolism. The city's cubic shape recalls the Holy of Holies in Solomon's Temple, which was also a perfect cube. This suggests that the entire city functions as the place of God's most intimate presence—what was once restricted to a single room is now expanded to encompass all of redeemed creation.

Similarly, the city's dimensions—12,000 stadia (about 1,400 miles)—communicate vastness using symbolic numbers. Twelve represents God's people (twelve tribes, twelve apostles), and 1,000 represents completeness. The message is clear: This city is large enough to accommodate all of God's people throughout history.

Perhaps most significant is what John doesn't see: "I did not see a temple in the city, because the Lord God Almighty and the Lamb are its temple." The temple represented God's presence with His people, but in the New Jerusalem, that presence is direct and unmediated. We will see God face to face.

The city also has no need for sun or moon because "the glory of God gives it light, and the Lamb is its lamp." This echoes Jesus' claim to be "the light of the world" (John 8:12) and fulfills Isaiah's prophecy: "The LORD will be your everlasting light, and your God will be your glory" (Isaiah 60:19).

NEW JERUSALEM GLORY (CONTINUED)

In chapter 22, the vision of the New Jerusalem continues with John seeing "the river of the water of life, as clear as crystal, flowing from the throne of God and of the Lamb down the middle of the great street of the city." This river recalls Ezekiel's vision of water flowing from the temple (Ezekiel 47:1-12) and Jesus' promise of "living water" (John 7:38).

On each side of the river stands the tree of life, bearing twelve crops of fruit, yielding its fruit every month. The leaves of the tree are for the healing of the nations. This image restores what was lost in Eden—access to the tree of life, which was blocked after the fall (Genesis 3:22-24). The monthly fruit suggests ongoing fruitfulness and abundance, while the healing leaves indicate the complete restoration of human relationships and societies.

CROSS REFERENCE: Paradise Restored

The New Jerusalem completes the story that began in Genesis, showing God's redemptive plan coming full circle:

Genesis 1–2 → Revelation 21–22

- God creates heaven and earth → New heaven and new earth
- Light created → God's glory provides light
- Water gathered, land appears → Sea (chaos) is no more
- Tree of life in garden → Tree of life in city
- Rivers flow from Eden → River flows from God's throne
- God walks with humans → God dwells with His people
- "No shame" (before sin) → "No curse" (after redemption)
- Mandate to rule creation → Saints reign forever

What Adam and Eve lost through sin, we regain in Christ—but in even greater measure. Eden was a garden; our final home is a city, representing not just pristine nature but perfected human culture and community.

Most wonderful of all, "The throne of God and of the Lamb will be in the city, and his servants will serve him. They will see his face, and his name will be on their foreheads." Seeing God's face represents the most intimate knowledge and fellowship possible. In the Old Testament,

such direct vision was impossible: "No one may see me and live" (Exodus 33:20). But in Christ, we will experience unhindered communion with God.

Having God's name on our foreheads symbolizes complete belonging and identity. We will be fully identified with God, sharing in His character and purpose. As John writes elsewhere, "We shall be like him, for we shall see him as he is" (1 John 3:2).

In this glorified state, "They will not need the light of a lamp or the light of the sun, for the Lord God will give them light. And they will reign for ever and ever." Light represents knowledge, joy, and life itself. Living in God's light means experiencing these blessings in their fullest measure, forever.

RIVER OF LIFE PROMISE

The river of life flowing from God's throne carries profound significance. Water sustains life, cleanses, and refreshes. Throughout Scripture, God promises living water to those who thirst for Him:

"Come, all you who are thirsty, come to the waters" (Isaiah 55:1).

"Whoever drinks the water I give them will never thirst. Indeed, the water I give them will become in them a spring of water welling up to eternal life" (John 4:14).

"Let the one who is thirsty come; and let the one who wishes take the free gift of the water of life" (Revelation 22:17).

This river represents the life-giving presence of the Holy Spirit, flowing from God to His people. Just as a river sustains a city, God's presence sustains His people eternally. The river's crystal clarity suggests perfect purity—no pollution, no contamination, nothing that diminishes life.

The description of the river also teaches us about eternal life. Many people misunderstand eternity as static and potentially boring. But the river suggests movement, freshness, and ongoing discovery. The monthly fruit from the tree of life indicates cycles of fruitfulness and new experiences. Eternal life isn't just endless duration but endless growth in our knowledge of God and enjoyment of His creation.

This river also fulfills our deepest thirsts. Augustine famously wrote, "You have made us for yourself, O Lord, and our hearts are restless until they rest in you." We spend our lives thirsting for what only God can provide—meaning, purpose, love, and belonging. In the New Jerusalem, these thirsts are fully satisfied.

And remarkably, this river is available to us now, though imperfectly. Jesus said, "Whoever believes in me, as Scripture has said, rivers of living water will flow from within them" (John 7:38, NIV). Through the indwelling Spirit, we experience a foretaste of the river of life that will flow in perfection in the new creation.

LIVING IN LIGHT OF HIS COMING

The closing verses of Revelation emphasize an urgent message: "Look, I am coming soon!" Three times in the final chapter (verses 7, 12, and 20), Jesus declares the imminence of His return. This repetition underscores the importance of living with an expectation of Christ's appearing.

"Blessed is the one who keeps the words of the prophecy written in this book" (22:7). This echoes the first blessing in 1:3, creating a frame around the entire book. Revelation isn't meant merely to satisfy our curiosity about the future but to shape how we live in the present.

"Look, I am coming soon! My reward is with me, and I will give to each person according to what they have done" (22:12). This reminds us that our actions matter eternally. While salvation is by grace through faith, not works, our works demonstrate the reality of our faith and determine our rewards in the kingdom.

The vision concludes with a stark warning: Those outside the city are "the dogs, those who practice magic arts, the sexually immoral, the murderers, the idolaters and everyone who loves and practices falsehood" (22:15). This isn't an exhaustive list of sins but represents attitudes and actions that reject God's rule. The "dogs" likely refer to false teachers who distort God's truth.

By contrast, Jesus identifies Himself as "the Root and the Offspring of David, and the bright Morning Star" (22:16). As David's root, He is David's source and Lord; as David's offspring, He is David's descendant and heir. The morning star heralds the dawn of a new day—Christ's return marks the dawn of God's new creation.

The Spirit and the bride say, "Come!" This invitation has two directions: We invite Christ to return quickly, and we invite thirsty souls to come to Christ for living water. The gospel invitation remains open: "Whoever is thirsty, let him come; and whoever wishes, let him take the free gift of the water of life" (22:17).

The book closes with a serious warning against adding to or taking away from "the words of the prophecy of this book" (22:18-19). This warns against both legalistic additions to God's requirements and liberal subtractions from His truth. God's Word is complete and sufficient; we must neither embellish it nor diminish it.

Jesus' final words in Scripture are, "Yes, I am coming soon." John responds with what should be the heartfelt cry of every believer: "Amen. Come, Lord Jesus" (22:20). This simple prayer expresses both faith in Christ's promise and yearning for its fulfillment.

OUR ETERNAL HOPE

The closing vision of Revelation provides several anchors for our hope:

First, we hope in God's presence. "Look! God's dwelling place is now among the people, and he will dwell with them" (21:3). Our deepest longing isn't for streets of gold or freedom from pain, but for unhindered communion with God Himself. Heaven is essentially God's space, and earth is human space; in the new creation, these realms unite as God dwells directly with His people.

Second, we hope in God's comfort. "He will wipe every tear from their eyes. There will be no more death or mourning or crying or pain" (21:4). God doesn't merely end suffering; He tenderly wipes away our tears. This intimate act of compassion shows that God doesn't just solve problems; He heals hearts.

Third, we hope in God's renewal. "I am making everything new!" (21:5). God doesn't discard creation and start over; He renews what was broken. The Greek word for "new" (kainos) emphasizes new quality, not new origin. God redeems rather than replaces His good creation.

Fourth, we hope in God's invitation. "To the thirsty I will give water without cost from the spring of the water of life" (21:6). God offers eternal life freely to all who recognize their thirst for Him. This matches Jesus' invitation: "Let anyone who is thirsty come to me and drink" (John 7:37).

Finally, we hope in God's victory. "He who was seated on the throne said, 'I am the Alpha and the Omega, the Beginning and the End'" (21:6). God initiated history, and He will bring it to its intended conclusion. Despite apparent chaos and evil, history moves purposefully toward God's predetermined goal.

This hope isn't just for the distant future. It transforms how we live today. When we know that God will wipe away every tear, we can face present suffering with courage. When we know that God is making all things new, we can participate in His renewing work now. When we know that Christ is coming soon, we can live with urgency and purpose.

As Peter writes, "Since everything will be destroyed in this way, what kind of people ought you to be? You ought to live holy and godly lives as you look forward to the day of God and speed its coming" (2 Peter 3:11–12, NIV). Our eternal hope doesn't lead to passive waiting but to active, holy living.

QUESTIONS FOR REFLECTION

1. How does understanding God's final judgment affect how you view the injustice in today's world?

2. In what ways does the vision of the New Jerusalem address your deepest longings? Which aspect of the eternal state most appeals to you?

3. How should the certainty of Christ's return influence your priorities and decisions today?

4. What does it mean for you personally to pray, "Come, Lord Jesus"? Do you find yourself longing for His return, or are you hesitant about it?

5. How might you "take the free gift of the water of life" more deeply in your current spiritual journey?

PRAYER RESPONSE

Sovereign Lord,

We stand in awe before Your perfect justice and boundless mercy. Thank You for providing a way of salvation through Christ, so that we need not fear the day of judgment but can anticipate it with joyful expectation.

We long for that day when You will wipe every tear from our eyes, when death and mourning, crying and pain will be no more. Until then, help us to live as citizens of the New Jerusalem even while we journey through this broken world.

Give us wisdom to recognize the counterfeit promises of Babylon and courage to come out from her influence. Strengthen our witness to those who haven't yet received the water of life, that they too might join the great multitude around Your throne.

And with John and all Your people throughout the ages, we pray: "Amen. Come, Lord Jesus!"

In the name of the One who is coming soon, Amen.

VICTORY DECLARATION

We stand confident today knowing that:

- God's judgment is perfectly just and true.
- Christ will return to establish His eternal kingdom.
- All evil will be decisively defeated.
- Creation will be renewed, not destroyed.
- God Himself will dwell among His people forever.
- Every tear will be wiped away.
- The water of life flows freely for all who thirst.

Therefore, we will live with joyful expectation, holy conduct, and faithful witness, knowing that our labor in the Lord is not in vain!

APPENDIX A

COMPLETE SYMBOL REFERENCE GUIDE

Numbers

- Seven: Completeness or perfection (seven churches, seven spirits, seven seals, seven trumpets, seven bowls)
- Six: Incompleteness or imperfection (666 = complete incompleteness)
- Four: Geographic completeness or the whole world (four living creatures, four corners of the earth)
- Twelve: Completeness of God's people (twelve tribes, twelve apostles, foundations, gates)
- Three: Perfect set, completeness, or finality (the Trinity; "holy, holy, holy")
- Ten: Perfection and totality (ten horns)
- Thousand: A vast number ("thousand thousand" = countless multitudes)
- 144,000: Complete number of God's people (12 x 12 x 1,000 = completeness x completeness x vastness)
- 666: The number of the beast—complete incompleteness, ultimate human rebellion
- 3½ years (42 months, 1,260 days): A limited period of suffering, persecution, or tribulation

Objects and Elements

- Throne: Sovereignty, rulership, and authority
- Crown (stephanos): Victory wreath or reward
- Crown (diadem): Royal authority
- Lampstand: Church or congregation
- Stars: Angels or messengers (often church leaders)
- Horns: Strength, power, or authority
- Eyes: Wisdom, insight, knowledge, or omniscience
- Sword: Word of God that judges and divides
- Scroll: God's purposes, plans, or decrees for history
- Seals: Security, authority, or ownership
- Trumpet: Warning, announcement, or call to action
- Censer: Prayers of the saints
- White Stone: Acquittal, acceptance, or victory

- Key: Authority to open or close, bind or loose
- Sea: Chaos, danger, or the masses of humanity
- Sea of Glass: Chaos tamed and under God's control
- Mountain: Kingdom, power, or stability
- Temple: God's dwelling place
- Altar: Sacrifice and worship
- Golden Bowls: Judgments of God's wrath
- New Name: Transformed identity and relationship

Colors

- White: Victory, purity, righteousness
- Red: Blood, war, violence
- Black: Famine, death, mourning
- Pale Green: Death, disease, decay
- Purple & Scarlet: Luxury, royalty, wealth, sin

Clothing and Appearance

- White Robes: Purity, victory, righteousness
- Fine Linen: Righteous deeds of God's people
- Sackcloth: Mourning, repentance, humility
- Nakedness: Shame, judgment, or spiritual poverty
- Golden Sash: Royal or priestly authority
- Hair White as Wool: Wisdom, eternality

Creatures and Figures

- Lamb: Christ as sacrifice and conqueror
- Lion: Christ as majestic king
- Dragon: Satan
- Beast from Sea: Political power against God
- Beast from Earth: False religion, propaganda, deception
- Woman Clothed with Sun: God's people (Israel/Church)
- Prostitute/Babylon: World system seducing God's people
- Bride/New Jerusalem: Redeemed people of God

- Four Living Creatures: Cherubim, the highest angelic beings
- Twenty-four Elders: Complete people of God (Old Testament and New Testament)
- Two Witnesses: Church in its prophetic role
- Locusts from the Pit: Demonic forces tormenting humanity

Places

- Babylon: World system opposed to God
- Egypt: Place of bondage and oppression
- Sodom: Moral corruption and judgment
- Wilderness: Testing, provision, and protection
- Mount Zion: God's presence and rule
- New Jerusalem: Perfected community of God's people
- Euphrates: Boundary between God's people and enemies
- Armageddon: Final battle between good and evil
- Lake of Fire: Final judgment and eternal separation

Actions

- Sealing: Divine protection or ownership
- Opening Seals: Revealing God's purposes
- Blowing Trumpets: Announcing judgment
- Pouring Bowls: Administering final judgment
- Standing: Victory or readiness
- Sitting: Authority or ruling
- Falling Down: Worship or defeat
- Casting Crowns: Attributing honor to God
- Marking: Allegiance or ownership

Natural Phenomena

- Earthquake: Divine intervention or upheaval
- Thunder/Lightning: God's power and presence
- Stars Falling: Cosmic upheaval, collapse of powers
- Sun Darkened: Judgment, end of an age
- Blood Moon: Judgment, catastrophe

Interpretive Keys

When interpreting these symbols, remember these principles:

1. Context is crucial: The same symbol may have different meanings in different contexts.
2. Biblical precedent matters: Many symbols in Revelation are drawn from the Old Testament and should be interpreted in that light.
3. Numbers are symbolic: Most numbers in Revelation convey theological meaning rather than literal quantities.
4. Consistency is important: Look for patterns in how symbols are used throughout Revelation.
5. Author's explanations take priority: When John explains a symbol, that interpretation should guide our understanding.
6. This reference guide provides a foundation for understanding Revelation's rich symbolic language, but always remember that the central message remains clear despite interpretive challenges: Jesus Christ is victorious, and those who remain faithful to Him will share in His eternal kingdom.

APPENDIX B

TIMELINE OF REVELATION EVENTS (IDEALIST VIEW)

The Idealist view interprets Revelation as depicting spiritual principles and patterns that repeat throughout history rather than predicting specific historical events in strict chronological sequence. This symbolic timeline presents how Revelation portrays the entire period between Christ's first and second comings.

First Coming of Christ

The Binding of Satan (Partially Fulfilled)

- Satan's ability to deceive the nations is limited when Jesus begins His ministry.
- The gospel is now able to spread to all nations. (Matthew 12:28-29; Revelation 20:1-3)
- Satan is not completely inactive but is "bound" in his ability to prevent the gospel's advance.

The Church Age (Present Time)

The Millennium (Revelation 20:4–6)

- Symbolizes the entire period between Christ's first and second comings
- Christ rules from heaven with believers who have died
- A time of both gospel advancement and persecution
- Not a literal 1,000 years but represents the complete period God has determined

Seven Churches (Revelation 2–3)

- Represent the complete spectrum of church life in every generation
- Churches experience various spiritual conditions simultaneously across history:
    - Faithfulness and persecution (Smyrna, Philadelphia)
    - Doctrinal correctness without love (Ephesus)
    - Compromise with culture (Pergamum, Thyatira)
    - Spiritual death despite reputation (Sardis)

- Self-sufficiency and lukewarmness (Laodicea)

Four Horsemen (Revelation 6:1–8)

- Ongoing realities throughout the church age:
  - White Horse: Conquest and deceptive power
  - Red Horse: War and civil conflict
  - Black Horse: Economic injustice and famine
  - Pale Horse: Death through various means

Seal, Trumpet, and Bowl Judgments (Revelation 6–16)

- Represent the same events from different perspectives with increasing intensity
- Each series follows this pattern:
  - First five judgments: Ongoing realities throughout history
  - Sixth judgment: What happens at history's end
  - Seventh judgment: Final judgment and beyond

The Two Witnesses (Revelation 11:1–14)

- Symbolize the church's prophetic testimony throughout history
- The pattern of faithful witness, apparent defeat, and vindication
- The 1,260 days represent the entire church age

The Woman and the Dragon (Revelation 12)

- The ongoing cosmic battle between Satan and God's people
- The protection of the church in the wilderness of this world
- Satan's continued attempts to destroy believers

The Beasts (Revelation 13)

- First Beast: Political power opposing God in every generation
- Second Beast: Religious deception and propaganda supporting the first beast
- The Mark of the Beast: Allegiance to anti-God systems in thought and action

Babylon the Great (Revelation 17–18)

- The seductive world system in every generation
- Economic, political, and religious forces opposed to God
- Prosperity built on compromise, idolatry, and injustice

End of the Age

Satan's Final Deception (Revelation 20:7–10)
- Satan released for "a little while" at the end of the church age
- The final gathering of the nations against God's people
- The last great persecution of the church

Armageddon (Revelation 16:12–16; 19:17–21)
- The final conflict between the forces of evil and Christ
- Not a literal battlefield but the decisive confrontation at Christ's return

Christ's Return (Revelation 19:11–16)
- Visible, personal return of Jesus
- The defeat of all evil powers
- The vindication of God's people

Final Judgment (Revelation 20:11–15)
- The great white throne judgment
- Resurrection of all the dead
- Judgment according to works
- Eternal destiny is determined by whether one's name is in the Book of Life

Eternal State

New Heaven and New Earth (Revelation 21–22)
- Complete restoration and transformation of creation
- No more sin, suffering, death, or tears
- God dwells directly with His people

New Jerusalem (Revelation 21:9–27)
- Perfected community of God's redeemed people
- Perfect fellowship with God
- Access to the Tree of Life
- Eternal reign with Christ

Key Principles of the Idealist Timeline

1. **Recapitulation:** The seven seals, seven trumpets, and seven bowls cover the same time period from different angles.

2. **Already/Not Yet:** Many prophecies have partial fulfillment now but await complete fulfillment at Christ's return.

3. **Progressive Intensification:** While the basic pattern of conflict repeats throughout history, there will be an intensification as the end approaches.

4. **Symbolic Time Periods:** Numbers like 1,260 days, 42 months, and "time, times, and half a time" represent the same limited but significant period of tribulation for God's people.

5. **Ultimate Focus:** Though Revelation describes patterns throughout history, its ultimate focus is on Christ's final victory and the eternal state.

This timeline helps us recognize that we live in the midst of Revelation's unfolding reality. The symbols and visions apply to our present circumstances while pointing toward the glorious consummation of all things in Christ.

APPENDIX C

MAPS AND CHARTS

The Seven Churches of Asia Minor

Church	Location	Status Today	Key Characteristics	Christ's Introduction	Promise to Overcomers
Ephesus	Western coast of Asia Minor, major port city	Ruins near modern Selçuk, Turkey	Doctrinally sound but loveless	Holds seven stars, walks among lampstands	Access to the Tree of Life
Smyrna	35 miles north of Ephesus	Modern Izmir, Turkey	Poor but spiritually rich, facing persecution	First and Last, died and came to life	Crown of life, not hurt by second death
Pergamum	40 miles north of Smyrna	Ruins near modern Bergama, Turkey	Faithful amid paganism, but compromising with culture	Has sharp two-edged sword	Hidden manna, white stone with new name
Thyatira	40 miles east of Pergamum	Modern Akhisar, Turkey	Growing in love and service, but tolerating false teaching	Eyes like fire, feet like bronze	Authority over nations, morning star
Sardis	30 miles southeast of Thyatira	Ruins near modern Sart, Turkey	Reputation for life but spiritually dead	Has seven spirits of God and seven stars	White garments, name in the Book of Life
Philadelphia	25 miles southeast of Sardis	Modern Alaşehir, Turkey	Faithful despite weakness, holding fast to Christ's name	Holy and true, has key of David	Pillar in God's temple, new name
Laodicea	40 miles southeast of Philadelphia	Ruins near modern Denizli, Turkey	Wealthy but lukewarm, self-sufficient	Amen, faithful witness, beginning of creation	Sit with Christ on His throne

The Four Views of Revelation

View	Timeline	Basic Approach	Strengths	Challenges
Preterist	Past	Most prophecies fulfilled by 70 AD (Jerusalem's destruction) or the fall of Rome	Strong emphasis on original historical context; Takes seriously "soon" language	May underestimate future fulfillment aspects; Can reduce relevance for today
Historicist	Progressive through history	Revelation forecasts entire church age with specific historical correspondences	Maintains relevance throughout church history; Views Scripture as applicable to all eras	Subjective correlations with historical events; Interpretations change with each generation
Futurist	Future	Most prophecies await future fulfillment, often in a 7-year tribulation	Takes apocalyptic language seriously; Maintains expectation of Christ's return	Can disconnect text from original audience; Often highly speculative
Idealist	Timeless principles	Sees Revelation as symbolic of the ongoing spiritual battle in every age	Applicable to all generations; Focuses on spiritual realities behind events	May miss specific historical fulfillments; Can become overly symbolic

The Three Sets of Judgments

Seven Seals	Seven Trumpets	Seven Bowls
Source: Opened by the Lamb	**Source:** Blown by angels	**Source:** Poured by angels
Target: 1/4 of the earth	**Target:** 1/3 of the earth	**Target:** Complete/total
Purpose: Initial warnings, beginning of sorrows	**Purpose:** Intensifying warning, call to repentance	**Purpose:** Final judgment, no more opportunity
First Four: Four horsemen: conquest, war, famine, death	**First Four:** Damage to land, sea, fresh water, heavens	**First Four:** Similar to trumpets but more severe
Fifth: Martyrs cry for justice	**Fifth:** Demonic torment	**Fifth:** Darkness and pain on beast's kingdom
Sixth: Cosmic upheaval, sealing of God's people	**Sixth:** Demonic army kills 1/3 of mankind	**Sixth:** Armageddon gathering
Seventh: Silence in heaven	**Seventh:** Kingdom proclaimed	**Seventh:** "It is done!" Final judgment
Interlude: Sealing of 144,000 and great multitude	**Interlude:** Little scroll and two witnesses	**Interlude:** None

The Structure of Revelation (Cyclical View)

- **PROLOGUE (1:1–8)**
  - **VISION OF CHRIST (1:9–20)**
  - **SEVEN CHURCHES (2:1–3:22)**
    - Ephesus (2:1–7)
    - Smyrna (2:8–11)
    - Pergamum (2:12–17)
    - Thyatira (2:18–29)
    - Sardis (3:1–6)
    - Philadelphia (3:7–13)
    - Laodicea (3:14–22)
  - **HEAVENLY THRONE ROOM (4:1–5:14)**
  - **SEVEN SEALS (6:1–8:1)**
    - First Six Seals (6:1–17)
    - INTERLUDE: 144,000 Sealed (7:1–8)
    - INTERLUDE: Great Multitude (7:9–17)
    - Seventh Seal (8:1)
  - **SEVEN TRUMPETS (8:2–11:19)**
    - First Six Trumpets (8:2–9:21)
    - INTERLUDE: Little Scroll (10:1–11)
    - INTERLUDE: Two Witnesses (11:1–14)
    - Seventh Trumpet (11:15–19)
  - **SEVEN SIGNS (12:1–14:20)**
    - Woman and Dragon (12:1–17)
    - Beast from Sea (13:1–10)
    - Beast from Earth (13:11–18)
    - Lamb and 144,000 (14:1–5)

- Three Angels (14:6–13)
- Harvest of the Earth (14:14–20)

SEVEN BOWLS (15:1–16:21)

- Preparation (15:1–8)
- Seven Bowls Poured Out (16:1–21)

FALL OF BABYLON (17:1–19:10)

- The Great Prostitute (17:1–18)
- Babylon's Fall (18:1–24)
- Rejoicing in Heaven (19:1–10)

FINAL VICTORY (19:11–20:15)

- Return of Christ (19:11–21)
- Millennium (20:1–6)
- Satan's Final Defeat (20:7–10)
- Great White Throne Judgment (20:11–15)

NEW CREATION (21:1-22:5)

- New Heaven and Earth (21:1–8)
- New Jerusalem (21:9–22:5)

EPILOGUE (22:6–21)

The Millennium: Three Main Views

Premillennialism	Postmillennialism	Amillennialism
Timeline: Christ returns → Millennium → Final Judgment	**Timeline:** Church age → Millennium → Christ returns → Final Judgment	**Timeline:** Church age (Millennium) → Christ returns → Final Judgment
Millennium Is: Literal 1,000-year reign of Christ on earth after His return	**Millennium Is:** Period of Christian influence and flourishing before Christ's return	**Millennium Is:** Symbolic of entire period between Christ's ascension and return
Nature: Visible, physical reign of Christ	**Nature:** Spiritual rule through the church	**Nature:** Spiritual rule of Christ from heaven
Christ's Return: Before the millennium	**Christ's Return:** After the millennium	**Christ's Return:** Ends the millennium
Satan's Binding: Occurs at Christ's second coming	**Satan's Binding:** Progressive binding through gospel advance	**Satan's Binding:** Occurred at Christ's first coming
Key Strengths: Takes 1,000 years literally; Clear separation of church and millennium	**Key Strengths:** Optimistic view of gospel's power; Motivates cultural engagement	**Key Strengths:** Consistent with "already/not yet" NT eschatology; Simplifies timeline
Variations: Historic Premillennialism, Dispensational Premillennialism	**Variations:** Postmillennial Reconstructionism, Theonomic Postmillennialism	**Variations:** Augustinian Amillennialism, Realized Amillennialism

The Unholy Trinity vs. The Holy Trinity

God the Father	God the Son	God the Holy Spirit	Counterfeit	Dragon (Satan)	Beast from the Sea	Beast from the Earth
Role: Source of authority Method: Warfare against God's people	Role: False messiah/ruler Method: Political power and intimidation	Role: Promotes worship of false messiah Method: Religious deception and propaganda	Characteristics: Seven heads, ten horns Downfall: Cast into lake of fire	Characteristics: Blasphemous names, fatal wound healed Downfall: Defeated at Christ's return	Characteristics: Looks like a lamb, speaks like a dragon Downfall: Exposed as false prophet	Goal: Receive worship due to Go

Geographic Map of the Seven Churches

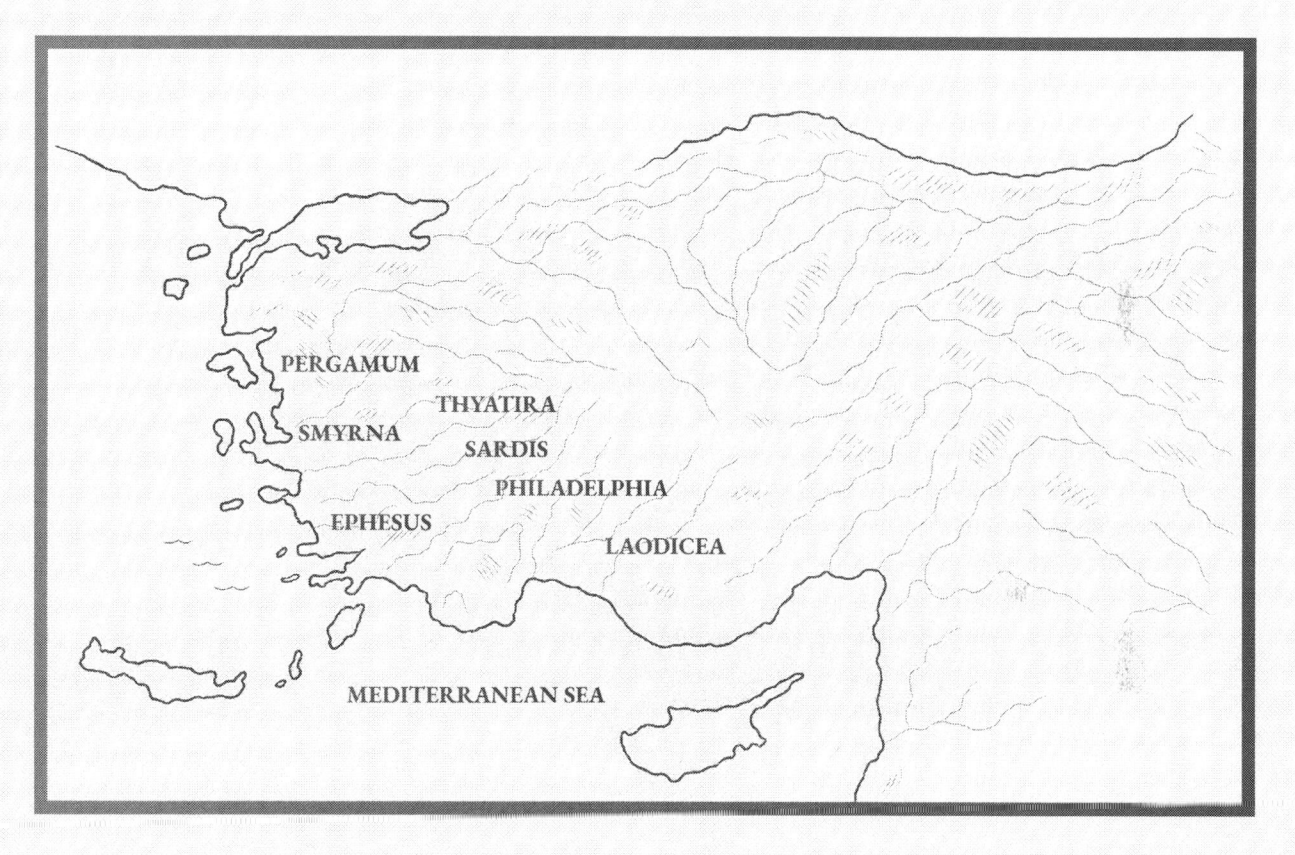

The Symbolic Timeline of Revelation (Idealist View)

FIRST COMING OF CHRIST
- Satan Bound (partially)
  - **CHURCH AGE/MILLENNIUM**
    - Seven Churches (various spiritual conditions)
    - Four Horsemen (ongoing realities)
    - Seal/Trumpet/Bowl Judgments (progressive intensity)
    - Two Witnesses (church testimony)
    - Woman protected in wilderness
    - Beasts and False Prophet active
    - Babylon the Great seducing nations
      - **END OF AGE**
        - Satan released briefly
        - Final deception/persecution
        - Armageddon
        - Christ's Return
          - **FINAL JUDGMENT**
            - Great White Throne
            - Books opened
            - Lake of Fire for wicked
              - **ETERNAL STATE**
                - New Heaven and Earth
                - New Jerusalem
                - God dwelling with His people

APPENDIX D

PERSONAL GROWTH RESOURCES

Extended Reflection Exercises

Spiritual Self-Assessment

Take time to reflect on which of the seven churches most closely resembles your current spiritual condition:

Ephesus (Revelation 2:1–7)

- Do I maintain strong doctrine but lack passionate love for Christ?
- Have I abandoned the love I had at first?
- Am I serving out of duty rather than devotion?
- Action step: Remember, repent, and return to your first works motivated by love.

Smyrna (Revelation 2:8–11)

- Am I facing persecution or hardship for my faith?
- Do I value spiritual riches above material wealth?
- Am I prepared to remain faithful even unto death?
- Action step: Take courage in Christ's promise of the crown of life.

Pergamum (Revelation 2:12–17)

- Am I remaining faithful in a difficult environment?
- Have I compromised with the culture in significant ways?
- Do I tolerate false teaching for the sake of peace?
- Action step: Repent of any compromises and stand firm on God's truth.

Thyatira (Revelation 2:18–29)

- Is my love, faith, service, and perseverance growing over time?
- Have I tolerated false teaching that leads to immoral behavior?
- Am I holding fast to what I have until Christ comes?
- Action step: Reject "deeper" teachings that contradict Scripture's moral standards.

Sardis (Revelation 3:1–6)

- Do I have a reputation for being spiritually alive while actually being dead?
- Are my works complete in God's sight?
- Have I soiled my garments through compromise?
- Action step: Wake up, strengthen what remains, remember what you received, and repent.

Philadelphia (Revelation 3:7–13)

- Am I maintaining faithfulness despite having little strength?
- Do I keep Christ's word and not deny His name?
- Am I holding fast to what I have?
- Action step: Continue in faithful endurance, knowing Christ opens doors no one can shut.

Laodicea (Revelation 3:14–22)

- Am I lukewarm in my commitment to Christ?
- Do I rely on material prosperity while being spiritually impoverished?
- Have I excluded Christ from areas of my life?
- Action step: Receive Christ's spiritual gold, white garments, and eye salve; open the door to renewed fellowship with Him.

Personal Inventory: The Beast's Influence

In what ways might the influence of the "beasts" from Revelation 13 be present in your life? Reflect honestly on the following:

1. **Authority Influences:** Which authorities in your life demand allegiance that might compete with your loyalty to Christ? (Government, employer, family expectations, cultural norms)

2. **Thought Patterns:** Where have you unconsciously adopted worldviews that contradict biblical teaching? (Materialism, individualism, relativism, secular humanism)

3. **Economic Pressures:** Have you ever compromised your faith for financial gain or security? In what situations do you feel pressure to "take the mark" to participate in economic life?

4. **Cultural Conformity:** What aspects of popular culture most tempt you to compromise your Christian witness? How might you be elevating human approval above God's?

5. **Deceptive Ideologies:** Which contemporary ideologies seem most "lamb-like" (appearing good and harmless) but actually speak with the "dragon's voice" (promoting anti-Christian values)?

Preparing for the Marriage Supper

The Bible portrays salvation as a wedding, with Christ as the Bridegroom and the church as His Bride. How are you preparing for this ultimate celebration?

1. **Devotion Assessment:** On a scale of 1–10, how would you rate your current devotion to Christ? What might increase your love for Him?

2. **Garment Preparation:** Revelation 19:8 says the Bride is clothed in "fine linen, bright and pure"—the righteous deeds of the saints. What specific "righteous deeds" is God calling you to?

3. **Invitation Extension:** Who in your life needs to hear about the invitation to the marriage supper of the Lamb? List 3–5 people and pray for opportunities to share with them.

4. **Anticipation Cultivation:** What practices might help you develop greater longing for Christ's return? (Scripture study, worship focused on Christ's return, fellowship with believers who share this hope)

Detailed Prayer Guides

Praying Through the Seven Letters

For Ephesus-like Seasons (When your love has grown cold)

Lord Jesus, forgive me for allowing my love for You to cool. I remember when my heart burned with passion for You and Your ways. Reignite that first love in me. Help me to serve You not from duty but from delight. Restore to me the joy of Your salvation, that I might do the works I did at first—not to earn Your favor but to express my love. Amen.

For Smyrna-like Seasons (When facing persecution)

Faithful One, as I face opposition for Your name's sake, fill me with courage. Remind me that You know my suffering and poverty, yet in You I am rich. Help me not to fear what I am about to suffer, whether it be ridicule, rejection, or worse. Give me faithfulness even unto death, that I may receive the crown of life. Let me remember that the One who died and came to life again walks with me through every trial. Amen.

For Pergamum-like Seasons (When tempted to compromise)

Lord of Truth, I live where Satan's throne is—surrounded by values and practices that oppose Your ways. Strengthen me to hold fast to Your name and not deny the faith. Forgive me for the times I've tolerated false teaching or compromised with worldly values. May Your sharp two-edged sword cut away all that does not please You in my life. Give me the hidden manna and write Your new name on my heart. Amen.

For Thyatira-like Seasons (When influenced by false teaching)

Jesus, whose eyes are like blazing fire, You see all that is in my heart. Thank You for the love, faith, service, and perseverance You've developed in me. Forgive me for tolerating teachings that lead to compromise. Help me discern truth from error, rejecting all that would lead me away from holiness. Give me the strength to hold fast until You come, that I may share in Your authority and receive the morning star. Amen.

For Sardis-like Seasons (When spiritually asleep)

Lord, You who hold the seven spirits of God and the seven stars, wake me from spiritual slumber. Though others may think I'm alive, You see my true condition. Strengthen what remains and is about to die. Help me remember what I received and heard; enable me to obey it and repent. Clothe me in white garments of purity and victory, and keep my name in the Book of Life. Make me watchful for Your return. Amen.

For Philadelphia-like Seasons (When serving faithfully with little strength)

Holy and True One, You have placed before me an open door that no one can shut. Though I have little strength, help me keep Your word and not deny Your name. Protect me from the hour of trial and make me a pillar in Your temple. Write upon me the name of Your God, of the New Jerusalem, and Your own new name. Until You come, help me hold fast to what I have, that no one may seize my crown. Amen.

For Laodicea-like Seasons (When lukewarm and self-sufficient)

Faithful and True Witness, forgive my lukewarm heart. I confess that I have said, "I am rich; I have acquired wealth and need nothing," not realizing I am wretched, pitiful, poor, blind, and naked. I receive Your counsel to buy from You gold refined in fire, white clothes to cover my shameful nakedness, and salve for my eyes. I hear You knocking and open the door of my heart. Come in and dine with me, that I may dine with You and overcome. Amen.

Praying Through the Throne Room (Revelation 4-5)

For a God-Centered Perspective

Holy, holy, holy Lord God Almighty, who was and is and is to come! Like the four living creatures, I bow before Your throne. When my world seems chaotic, remind me that You reign supreme. When evil appears to triumph, show me the sea of glass—chaos tamed before Your throne. When I'm tempted to worry about tomorrow, help me see the twenty-four elders casting their crowns before You, acknowledging Your sovereignty over all. Amen.

For Worship That Honors the Lamb

Worthy is the Lamb who was slain! Lord Jesus, You alone could take the scroll and open its seals. By Your blood, You purchased people from every tribe, language, people, and nation. Help me worship You not based on how I feel but on who You are and what You've done. May my life declare Your worth to everyone I meet. You are worthy to receive power and wealth and wisdom and strength and honor and glory and praise! Amen.

For Participation in Heaven's Worship

God of Glory, as the elders cast their crowns before Your throne, I surrender all my achievements, possessions, and abilities to You. Everything I have comes from You and belongs to You. Unite my worship with the heavenly chorus. When I gather with Your people, remind me that we join with angels, living creatures, and saints from every age in declaring Your worth. May my earthly worship be a rehearsal for eternity. Amen.

Praying for Protection from Deception

Against the Dragon's Lies

Father of Truth, Satan is the father of lies and has been deceiving the world since the beginning. By the blood of the Lamb, silence his accusations against me. When he tells me I've failed too much to be useful to You, remind me that there is no condemnation for those in Christ Jesus. When he whispers that You don't really love me, show me the cross. When he suggests Your ways are too restrictive, reveal the freedom found in obedience. Expose his schemes and keep me grounded in Your truth. Amen.

Against the Beasts' Demands

Lord Jesus, in a world that demands allegiance to many things, help me reserve ultimate loyalty for You alone. When political powers overreach, give me the wisdom to render to Caesar only what is Caesar's and to God what is God's. When cultural pressures mount, strengthen me to stand firm rather than conform. When economic systems require compromise to participate, provide alternative paths or the courage to accept exclusion. May Your name, not the beast's mark, be written on my mind and actions. Amen.

Against Babylon's Seduction

Holy Spirit, Babylon surrounds me with its glittering attractions and empty promises. When materialism whispers "more," remind me that life does not consist in the abundance of possessions. When comfort becomes my idol, recall to my mind the way of the cross. When status beckons, show me Jesus, who made Himself nothing. When instant gratification tempts me, turn my eyes to eternal rewards. Help me come out from Babylon and not share in her sins, that I may not share in her plagues. Amen.

VICTORY JOURNAL TEMPLATE

Daily Reflection Framework

Scripture Reading Today: _____ Date: _____

What I Learned About:

God's Character:
_____
_____
_____

Satan's Tactics:
_____
_____
_____

The Church's Mission:
_____
_____
_____

Christ's Return:
_____
_____
_____

Where I See the Four Horsemen at Work Today:
_____
_____
_____
_____
_____

Where I Notice Babylon's Influence:
_____
_____
_____
_____
_____

How I Maintained My Witness:

Prayer of Victory:

Tomorrow's Battle Plan:

WEEKLY OVERCOMER ASSESSMENT

Complete this assessment at the end of each week:

1. **Spiritual Alertness:** On a scale of 1–10, how aware was I of spiritual warfare this week?
   _____

2. **Victories Celebrated:** List specific instances where you overcame temptation, maintained your witness, or experienced God's victory:
   - _____
   - _____
   - _____

3. **Areas of Struggle:** Where did I compromise or face defeat this week?
   - _____
   - _____
   - _____

4. **What God Showed Me:** What new insights about the cosmic battle did I gain?
   - _____
   - _____

5. **Scripture That Strengthened Me:** Which verses particularly helped me stand firm?
   - _____

6. **Prayer for the Week Ahead:** Based on this week's experiences, what specific victory am I praying for?
   - _____

Recommended Resources for Deeper Study

Books on Revelation

- Revelation For You by Tim Chester
- Exalting Jesus in Revelation by Daniel L. Akin
- Revelation: A Manual of Spiritual Warfare by Max Doner
- Interpreting Apocalyptic Literature: An Exegetical Handbook (Handbooks for Old Testament Exegesis) by Richard Taylor

Online Resources

- https://www.theologyforyou.com/16-how-to-study-apocalyptic-literature/
- https://learn.ligonier.org/articles/how-to-read-apocalyptic-literature
- https://www.thegospelcoalition.org/essay/introduction-to-old-testament-apocalyptic-literature/

Study Methods for Revelation

- **Symbolic Tracing:** Track specific symbols (e.g., lamb, throne, seals) throughout Revelation and related Scriptures
- **Parallel Reading:** Read Revelation alongside related Old Testament prophetic books (Daniel, Ezekiel, Zechariah)
- **Devotional Approach:** Focus on one vision or image each day for personal application
- **Theological Mapping:** Identify major theological themes (e.g., God's sovereignty, Christ's victory, faithful witness) and trace their development
- **Historical Context Study:** Research the Roman Empire, emperor worship, and early church persecution to better understand the book's setting

Remember that the goal of studying Revelation is not merely to acquire academic knowledge, but to experience transformed living. As you engage with these resources and methods, continue to ask: "How does this truth call me to greater faithfulness, endurance, and hope in Christ?"